Classics in the Classroom

How did they command such deference—English teachers? Compared with the men who taught physics and biology, what did they really know of the world? It seemed to me, and not only to me, that they knew what was most worth knowing.

Tobias Wolff, "Class Picture"

The process of reading is not a half-sleep; but in the highest sense an exercise, a gymnastic struggle; that the reader is to do something for himself.

Walt Whitman

Classics in the Classroom

Designing Accessible Literature Lessons

Carol Jago

HEINEMANN
Portsmouth, NH

Heinemann
A division of Reed Elsevier Inc.
361 Hanover Street
Portsmouth, NH 03801–3912
www.heinemann.com

Offices and agents throughout the world

The author and publisher wish to thank those who have generously given permission to reprint borrowed material:

Excerpts of the article "The National Writing Project: A Best Idea from James Gray" by Carol Jago from *Voices from the Middle*, May 2003, appear in Chapter 6. Copyright © 2003 by the National Council of Teachers of English. Reprinted with permission.

"Penelope" from *The World's Wife* (1999) by Carol Ann Duffy is reprinted by permission of Macmillan Publishers Ltd.

Library of Congress Cataloging-in-Publication Data
Jago, Carol, 1951–
     Classics in the classroom : designing accessible literature lessons / Carol Jago.
         p. cm.
Includes bibliographical references and index.
     ISBN 0-325-00590-7 (acid-free paper)
     1. American literature—Study and teaching (Secondary)—United States.
     2. English literature—Study and teaching (Secondary)—United States.
     3. Homer—Study and teaching (Secondary)—United States. I. Title.
     PS47.U6J34 2004
     810'.71'273—dc22   2003022874

Editor: Lisa Luedeke
Production: Elizabeth Valway
Interior design: Judy Arisman
Cover design: Jenny Jensen Greenleaf
Composition: Argosy
Manufacturing: Steve Bernier

Printed in the United States of America on acid-free paper
08 07 06 05 04 RRD 1 2 3 4 5

To my mother, Mary Crosetto, who said I was "never any problem as a child. You always had a book." Thanks for all those trips to the library.

Contents

Introduction

Literature Instruction at a Crossroads

SOMEWHERE AROUND PAGE 284 of *The Grapes of Wrath,* even the most dedicated of English teachers often lose momentum and faith in the text. The students are whining. You have spent weeks on the book and no one likes it. Half the class isn't keeping up with the reading. You worry that the other half is reading the SparkNotes. At the video store you gaze guiltily at the Gary Cooper movie. Just as you are about to abandon ship, you reread this paragraph:

> And the companies, the banks worded at their own doom and they did not know it. The fields were fruitful, and starving men moved on the roads. The granaries were full and the children of the poor grew up rachitic, and the pustules of pellagra swelled on their sides. The great companies did not know that the line between hunger and anger is a thin line. And money that might have gone to wages went for gas, for guns, for agents and spies, for blacklists,

for drilling. On the highways the people moved like ants and searched for work, for food. And the anger began to ferment. (Steinbeck 1999, 284)

Suddenly you remember why you love teaching literature and what keeps you in this crazy profession. You remind yourself that it doesn't matter whether or not sixteen-year-olds say they "like" a book. What matters is that they read it and consider what can happen when poverty pushes a family past endurance. Books like *The Grapes of Wrath* have the power to shape lives. The problem is that most teenagers don't want their lives to be "shaped" by someone not of their own choosing. This is why I will argue that teachers shouldn't always give young readers a choice. John Steinbeck forces you to consider the lives of people other than yourself in circumstances different from your own. He demands that you stand barefoot with Ma Joad:

Ma was heavy, but not fat; thick with childbearing and work. She wore a loose Mother Hubbard of gray cloth in which there had once been colored flowers, but the color was washed out now, to that the small flowered pattern was only a little lighter gray than the background. The dress came down to her ankles, and her strong, broad, bare feet moved quickly and deftly over the floor. (74)

I call this experience "education."

I will be the first to admit that teaching classics like The *Grapes of Wrath* or the rich, complex works of Mary Shelley, Fyodor Dostoyevsky, Ralph Ellison, Toni Morrison, or Gabriel García Márquez is not easy. Guiding young people through these books is the work of heroes, of champions. Of course kids will complain. The reading is difficult and there are many pages to go before they sleep. Popular culture is seductive and generally anti-intellectual. For a teacher to persist—sometimes coaxing, sometimes driving—requires an act of will. On the pages that follow I make a case for the importance of teaching powerful literature and offer methods for teaching novels, plays, and poems that are not "easy reads." Simply assigning books is not enough; teachers need to have an instructional plan that makes difficult texts accessible to students.

Next year will be my thirtieth year in the classroom. During that time I will have taught seventh through twelfth grades, all of them in the Santa Monica Malibu Unified School District. The high school where I now teach enrolls 3,400 students from a broad range of ethnic and socioeconomic backgrounds. Over fifty languages are spoken on campus. Movie stars' children sit in class next to homeless children. One-third of the students are on free or subsidized lunch. In many ways ours is a bipolar school with large numbers of students scoring in the very top percentiles on standardized tests and equally large numbers of students scoring at the very bottom. I believe all these students deserve the riches that great literature offers. It can help us understand both the world and one another.

Carol Jago

1

Seven Guiding Principles for Literature Teachers

1. STUDENTS MUST READ

The statement that students must read in order to study literature seems obvious, but a peek inside many middle and high school English classes may persuade you why we must begin with this dictum. Too many students are doing everything *but* reading. Common nonreading activities include:

- drawing storyboards
- performing scenes
- watching films
- painting murals
- designing book jackets

While these projects may help to engage students in their reading, they must be used sparingly and should always be accompanied by a writing assignment. Classroom time is precious. Learning suffers when teachers squander it by taking a full class period for seventeen-year-olds to play with markers and poster board.

Students should be working in Vygotsky's Zone of Proximal Development. Ideally instruction is aimed at the level where students can learn with the aid of a teacher or more knowledgeable peers (Vygotsky 1962). The texts chosen for classroom study should be ones that students are unable to read without you. In too many cases middle and high school instruction is aimed at what I call the ZME, the Zone of Minimal Effort. In this instructional zone, the texts are as short as possible; if possible, humorous; every day's lesson stands alone to eliminate reliance on students' doing homework reading; and basic skills are retaught *ad nauseam.* While I understand how student absences and the lack of enabling skills causes teachers to work in this Zone of Minimal Effort, under such conditions reading skills do not improve. While seemingly responsive to student needs, this kind of instruction, in fact, leaves students who are working below grade level farther and farther behind.

The Consortium on Chicago School Research observed thousands of hours of instruction in Chicago's urban and suburban public schools and found that in high-poverty classrooms a pattern of repeated instruction was the norm (Smith, Smith, and Bryk 1998). One day, two researchers at the same school emerged from third- and eighth-grade classrooms only to discover that they had both observed similar lessons on how to write a paragraph. Many skills need to be revisited and reinforced over time, but the repetition of low-level instruction with little or no development in terms of complexity is troubling indeed. Comparing two literature lessons—one in fifth grade on *Charlotte's Web,* another in tenth grade on the Rudolfo Anaya novel *Bless Me, Ultima*—researchers found few differences apart from the literature itself. In both classrooms students:

- read much of the book aloud in class;

- took quizzes with "who, what, where, when" questions referring to the basic facts of the story;
- discussed the theme, which had been determined by the teacher (friendship in *Charlotte's Web* and superstition in *Bless Me, Ultima*); and
- spent several weeks to write one draft of a short paper on the book. (7)

I would argue that this is quite a low level of instruction for fifth graders, but to think that sixteen-year-olds are still focusing on basic story elements rather than exploring the various themes within a rich piece of literature or learning how to draw inferences from the text goes a long way to explain why these students score poorly on standardized tests. They haven't had any practice with analysis. They haven't been taught how to do what their state standards and the test in front of them demand.

Of course, not all students are similarly shortchanged. In Chicago, researchers found that at integrated schools in middle-class neighborhoods the content of instruction, grade by grade, was for the most part consistent with the content of the test. Yet this was not the case in predominately minority and African American or high-poverty schools. In these schools, by the eighth grade there was on average a three- to five-grade-level gap between instructional content and test content. This means that children are being tested on skills and material they have never seen. At my high school we find a similar gap between instruction in "regular" classes and honors classes. With over a third of the ninth- and tenth-grade class enrolled in honors courses, the level of instruction in regular classes too often sinks to the Zone of Minimal Effort. That honors classes are largely made up of white and Asian students while regular classes are made up of Latino and African American students makes this a critical issue on campus.

Whatever their ethnicity or socioeconomic status, students who attend schools with a coherent curriculum aligned with state standards are much less likely to repeat the same instructional material year after year. Lev Vygotsky wrote, "the only good kind of instruction is that which marches ahead of development and leads it" (1962, 104). Instead of looking for ways to get through the day without student complaints about the texts being too hard or boring, teachers must develop lessons that create scaffolding for reading rich literature. Students who read below grade level and English language learners need to read more, not less, than their peers in honors classes.

2. DON'T CONFUSE READING FOR PLEASURE WITH THE STUDY OF LITERATURE

I have a love/hate relationship with young adult literature. On the one hand I adore reading books like these. I am addicted to popular mysteries and thrillers that allow me to indulge in the visceral pleasure of reading. I turn pages quickly, skimming along at a breakneck pace to find out what happens next. I recognize characters that remind me of people I know and who have problems just like mine. Best of all I can finish reading the slim volume in a single sitting. How could I deny my students such pleasure? The hundreds of spy thrillers and police stories I have read have clearly expanded my background knowledge of the world and the habit of moving quickly through a text has undoubtedly improved my reading fluency. On the other hand, if these are the only kinds of books students are reading in school, they simply haven't studied literature.

The mistake we have made is to confuse this kind of pleasure reading with the study of literature. With so many students hardly reading anything at all, it seems preferable to have them read something rather than nothing. While this point is well taken, I would argue that classical literature possesses qualities that popular fiction does not. *Crime and Punishment* has the power to change young readers' lives. As students begin to identify with Raskolnikov, they explore the duality within us all and our capacity for great good and great evil. Dostoyevsky is a master storyteller. So are Ralph Ellison and Gabriel García Márquez. But their books are long and difficult to read. Like the study of geometry or the study of physics, the study of literature is demanding of the reader. That is no reason to abandon it.

I believe that students' reading lives should include two very different kinds of books. One kind acts as a mirror—reflecting students' own experiences with peers, parents, sex, drugs, and school. Young people need stories in which someone who looks and thinks as they do has handled these problems, for better and for worse. Apart from a lively book talk to interest them in picking up the volume, teenagers shouldn't need a teacher's help with "mirror" books. In fact, our penchant for discussions about foreshadowing, symbolism, and themes tends to ruin such stories for kids.

Students also need books that act as windows. These stories offer readers access to other worlds, other times, other cultures. Few young people think they have much in common with Odysseus until an artful teacher helps them see how we are all on a journey toward self-discovery. Few relate to Pip until they walk for a while in Dickens' fictional world and begin to understand their own great expectations. Students need both kinds of books. Of course, teenagers need help looking through the window of most classical texts. Left on their own they can only see through it darkly. These books seem opaque, full of incomprehensible references and unfamiliar language. It is the teacher's job and the purpose of instruction to clear that window so that students can peer through.

Oprah Winfrey is offering us a helping hand. After promoting pleasure reading for five years through Oprah's Book Club, Oprah is now hosting "Traveling with the Classics." As Anna Quindlen said of this idea, "All reading is good reading. And all reading of Jane Austen and Charles Dickens is sublime reading" (Zanoza 2003, 13). Oprah's first selection was John Steinbeck's *East of Eden,* the brutal story of two families whose successive generations re-create the fatal rivalry of Cain and Abel in California's Salinas Valley. When Oprah's choice was announced the *Chicago Tribune* ran a count/counterpoint feature with staff reporters arguing for and against her taking up classical literature as a new domain. The arguments against the new book club smacked of sour grapes. Why fear that Oprah's publicity machine will dumb down Steinbeck? As long as people are reading the book—and with Penguin, Steinbeck's publisher, ordering 600,000 extra copies and the book topping the *New York Times* paperback bestseller list, one assumes that they are—there is little danger of damage to the novel. *East of Eden* was a bestseller when it appeared in 1952. The more readers who discover the pleasure that can come from reading classical literature, the less likely they will be to settle for second-rate stories.

3. DON'T SIMPLY ASSIGN DIFFICULT BOOKS; TEACH THEM

If there was ever a Golden Age for English teachers, when we could hand out books, assign homework reading, and begin class with "So what do you think?" I missed it. In the twenty-nine years I have spent in middle and high school, I have never taught such a class. I'm not complaining; I just don't think teenagers respond favorably to such instruction. It is their nature to do as little as possible and our job to help them do as much as possible. The tension will always exist. Good teachers know how to work with it. Their students thank them for it in June. The study of literature requires a subtle interplay of classroom tasks that scaffold difficult texts.

Many well-intentioned teachers have abandoned the classics in favor of what they think will be more user-friendly titles. This is a mistake. That students can't read a book on their own doesn't mean that, with help, they can't and shouldn't read it. Instead of choosing more seemingly "relevant" stories, we should be showing students how classic heroes struggle with the very same monsters we face today. If I were in charge of the world, I would mandate that every ninth grader read Robert Louis Stevenson's *The Strange Case of Dr. Jekyll and Mr. Hyde.* How better to help young people consider the evil that lurks within us all? The short novel is rich and layered, unfolding like a mystery story. Teachers shouldn't be put off by the fear that many students would find the text difficult. I have stopped telling students as I hand out books that they are going to love this text and instead tell them that what they are about to read may at first seem quite hard. I even warn them that, at first, they may hate it. I promise to help them through and also assure them that in my professional opinion, they will ultimately feel that the struggle was worthwhile.

Stevenson's first sentence describes the story's narrator, the dour Mr. Utterson:

> Mr. Utterson the lawyer was a man of rugged countenance, that was never lighted by a smile; cold, scanty and embarrassed in discourse; backward in sentiment; lean, long, dusty, dreary, and yet somehow lovable. (1979, 29)

I invite students to think about why it is rational that this tale of extraordinary horror be told by such an utterly reliable narrator. I also help them negotiate Stevenson's complex sentences. We talk about his word choice and define unfamiliar vocabulary. Together we picture Victorian London in our minds' eyes. I call this teaching.

It seems wrong to me that schools should reserve the classics for honors students. Ignoring the elitism that such a curricular decision betrays, teachers defend a watered-down reading list for "regular" students by explaining to themselves and others that most teenagers can't understand the difficult vocabulary. Besides, they argue, today's kids won't read anything that is old. I worry that in our determination to provide students with literature they "relate to" we end up teaching works that students actually don't need much help with. And I worry that we do this at the expense of teaching classics that they most certainly do need assistance negotiating. This is not to suggest that we stop putting contemporary literature into students' hands, but only to remind ourselves that we should be teaching in Vygotsky's Zone of Proximal Development and not the Zone of Minimal Effort. If students can read a book on their own, if this is a mirror book, it probably isn't the best choice for classroom study. Classroom texts should pose intellectual challenges to young readers. These texts should be books that will make students stronger readers, stronger people for having studied them. Effective literature study requires that teachers recognize and address in their lessons the aspects of classical literature that make it challenging for their students. Assigning books isn't enough. We need to teach them.

4. READING LITERATURE REQUIRES LANGUAGE STUDY AND BUILDS VOCABULARY

Teachers most frequently decide that a book is too hard because they believe the vocabulary is beyond students' ken. Instead of helping students build vocabulary as they read, some teachers keep looking for easier books with fewer big words. I know. I've gone down this path myself and found it to be a dead end. My reluctant readers—the ones who can but won't read—still thought these high-interest, easy-reading books were boring and hard. They still didn't do their homework. For me to invest instructional time on a text, I need to be convinced that the book will be worth students' time in terms of complex, engaging content. If this means that students are going to have to learn new words in order to read these books, so much the better.

Most young adult literature relies heavily on dialogue to carry the plot. This not only makes the text appear less dense and daunting but also results in the book being impoverished in vocabulary. In conversation few of us use more than a fraction of the words we know. Given that the dialogue in most young adult novels involves teenagers talking to other teenagers, the breadth and range of vocabulary in these books is particularly limited. As my students might say, "I ike, don't even go there." Novels that use dialogue at the expense of description and detail do little to build students' academic language.

If you are in any doubt that most students are in desperate need of targeted instruction in vocabulary, take a look at the research on comparative vocabularies:

- Three-year-olds from professional homes know twice as many words as parents from families on welfare. (Hart and Risley 2003, 7)
- First-grade children from higher socioeconomic groups know about twice as many words as lower socioeconomic children. (Graves, Burnetti, and Slater 1982)
- High-performing twelfth graders know about four times as many words as their low-performing peers. (Smith 1941)
- Lowest-performing twelfth graders have vocabularies about equal to high-knowledge third graders. (Smith 1941)

If these findings haven't depressed you enough, Hart and Risley discovered that once established, the pattern and rate at which children build language and develop vocabulary is difficult to alter. Those who come to school with rich vocabularies thrive; those who arrive with a language gap never seem to make up the difference.

The good news is that instruction can make a difference. In an outstanding book that should be mandatory for every teacher, *Bringing Words to Life: Robust Vocabulary Instruction,* Isabel Beck, Margaret McKeown, and Linda Kucan describe instructional methods that help students bridge this language gap and begin to negotiate texts that might otherwise seem outside their zone of proximal development. In the next chapter I offer specific guidelines for developing students' vocabulary within the context of classical literature.

5. READING LITERATURE BUILDS BACKGROUND KNOWLEDGE

When an excerpt from Jack London's *White Fang* appeared on California's 2001 exit exam, many teachers argued that their urban students didn't have the background information to read the passage. They felt the choice of such literature for a high-stakes exam prejudiced their students' chances of success. At first I nodded in agreement. It made sense that a lack of background knowledge about the Alaskan wilderness would inhibit students' comprehension of *White Fang.* Then I thought some more. I have never traveled to the Alaskan wild or had a single experience with wolves. Where did I accumulate the "background knowledge" needed to visualize London's fictional world? From books, particularly a string of dead dog stories I read when I was about ten.

Without question background knowledge facilitates reading comprehension. You have only to turn to a section of the newspaper that you don't commonly read to see how your own comprehension drops when the context is unfamiliar and the vocabulary unique to the context. An article in the *New York Times* titled "Bets in Both Directions Help a Fund Look Good" (on a page I do not typically read on any given Sunday), concludes with the following paragraph:

But the fund hasn't always beaten the index. The portfolio matched the performance of the S. & P.'s in 1998 and 1999 but underperformed it in 1997, when the fund's total return was 19.1 percent and the S. & P.'s was 33.4 percent. The underperformance relative to the S. & P. during those bull-market years was substantial. But the fund's performance in those years does not look bad in hindsight, especially given the returns since then. (Fuerbringer 2003)

There is not a single word here that I don't know, yet I find the passage most difficult to understand. I know what an index looks like in a book, but this "index" obviously refers to something else. "Fund" is a simple word, but this use of it falls outside my experience. I know that S. & P. refers to Standard & Poor's but couldn't tell for the life of me what they do or how they do it. I can manage to grasp the gist of this writer's point if I reread and tap my memory of what I've heard but never paid much attention to on the *Nightly Business Report* while waiting for *The News Hour*. A fluent reader of the business pages I am not.

I want to argue that what I need to become a better reader of the business pages is not a trip to Wall Street. To improve my reading comprehension I need to read about investment in the business section every day. Repeated exposure to familiar words in new contexts will deepen my understanding of specialized vocabulary. As my word knowledge grows, my background knowledge about finance will expand. Over time my reading comprehension and fluency might begin to approach the level at which I read the book review section, a portion of the Sunday paper I have read with loving care for thirty years.

You are able to read this book with comprehension and ease because you are familiar with the world of the classroom, both from your experience as a teacher as well as from your experience reading other books about teaching. Background knowledge clearly makes a difference in comprehending what we read. At the same time reading is the best way to build background knowledge. The more you read, the more you know. If the only stories students read are ones set in their own time and their own milieu, how will they ever know the rest of the world? How will they know history? Field trips will not repair that shortcoming. Wider reading of classical world literature may do so.

Once when a class of tenth graders was reading Victor Hugo's *The Hunchback of Notre Dame,* I worried that they would find the opening scene utterly incomprehensible. To help them visualize the time and place I showed the first few minutes of the 1939 film. The moment Charles Laughton as Quasimodo poked his grotesque head out the window, I hit STOP. Those few pictures gave them just enough background information, triggering their own imaginations, to be able to construct subsequent scenes on their own. We never went back to watch the rest of the movie. Instead we moved on to reading the next book.

6. READING LITERATURE EDUCATES STUDENTS' IMAGINATIONS

Good literature is disturbing. It forces readers to examine the lives of others objectively from the inside out. It educates our imaginations by engaging our emotions in powerful stories that affect us viscerally. In the opening scene of Richard Wright's *Native Son,* a reader senses what it is like to be Bigger Thomas killing the rat that has invaded his family's one-room apartment. We feel his fear as the rat tears his trouser leg and then shudder with loathing when Bigger dangles the dead rat in his sister's face and makes her faint. We begin to see how Bigger brutalizes others in order to hide his own fear. It is an awful spectacle to watch. Yet Wright's compelling narrative defies us to look away.

Wright wrote *Native Son* in 1940 to draw attention to the plight of young black men in America, a generation of Biggers for whom violence against other human beings had become the most appropriate response to the disastrous conditions of their lives.

> "I *could* fly a plane if I had a chance," Bigger said.
> "If you wasn't black and if you had some money and if they'd let you go to that aviation school, you *could* fly a plan," Gus said.
> For a moment Bigger contemplated all the "ifs" that Gus had mentioned. Then both boys broke into hard laughter, looking at each other through squinted eyes. When their laughter subsided, Bigger said in a voice that was half-question and half-statement:
> "It's funny how the white folks treat us, ain't it?"
> "It better be funny," Gus said.
> "Maybe they right in not wanting us to fly," Bigger said. "'Cause if I took a plane up I'd take a couple of bombs along and drop 'em sure as hell. . . ."
> They laughed again, still looking upwards. The plane sailed and dipped and spread another word against the sky: GASOLINE. . . .
> "Use Speed Gasoline," Bigger mused, rolling the words slowly from his lips. "God, I'd like to fly up there in that sky." (1979, 17)

As students read this exchange between Bigger and Gus, they consider what it would feel like to have no options, no chance of a better life, no hope of ever being able to achieve one's dreams. The miracle of Wright's novel is that it keeps readers in Bigger's corner when every human instinct and all common sense urges us to label the character a monster.

Powerful literary experiences expose young people to the complexity of the world around them. Why is Bigger so mean? How can the Daltons have so much when Bigger's family has nothing? Could Mrs. Dalton be blind in more than one way? Working through the novel, readers practice dealing with impossible situations. Why didn't Bigger just admit killing Mary was an accident? How can he be so horrible to his girlfriend? Students begin to discover that great literature doesn't offer simple solutions. Think of Oedipus.

Reading is not a vaccine for small-mindedness, but it does make it difficult to think only of one's self and one's own comfortable little world. If one purpose of public education is to prepare students for the complex responsibilities of citizenship, I can think of no better preparation for these responsibilities than reading the works of this country's naturalist writers: Stephen Crane, Jack London, Frank Norris, Theodore Dreiser, and Upton Sinclair. These novelists held that man's character and behavior are entirely determined by heredity and environment. As M. H. Abrams explains, "A person inherits compulsive instincts—especially hunger, the drive to accumulate possessions, and sexuality—and is then subject to the social and economic forces in the family, the class, and the milieu into which that person is born" (1999, 261). The conclusion of a naturalistic novel is "tragic" but not in the familiar Shakespearean sense where a hero loses in his battle with the gods or fate. Bigger Thomas "is a pawn to multiple compulsions, usually disintegrates, or is wiped out." Not much chance of a happy ending.

The more my students tell me that they don't need these depressing stories—thinking to themselves that their future as a lawyer, CEO, or financial consultant is bright—the more I tell them to read. Literature creates empathy and without empathy there can be little hope of a civilized society. These young people may someday be voting in the U.S. Senate on whether or not to go to war. They need to have experienced the harshness of battle with Stephen Crane, Norman Mailer, and Tim O'Brien. They may someday sit on a jury in a murder trial. They need to know what it is like to be Bigger Thomas.

In her book *Poetic Justice,* Martha Nussbaum (1995) writes about her experience as a visiting professor in law and literature at the University of Chicago Law School. As the school is located within spitting distance of the neighborhood where Bigger lived, she and her students were uniquely positioned to examine the relevance of Wright's novel, an imaginative piece of literature, for their law studies. Nussbaum discovered that "what was being sought from such teaching was the investigation and principled defense of a humanistic and multi-valued conception of public rationality that is powerfully exemplified in the common-law tradition" (xv). The University of Chicago had determined that for these future attorneys and future judges to be fully prepared for the work that lay ahead, they needed to educate their imaginations. Along with *Native Son*, they read Charles Dickens' *Hard Times* and E. M. Forster's *Maurice*. Nussbaum argues that "if we do not cultivate the imagination in this way, we lose, I believe, an essential bridge to social justice. If we give up on 'fancy,' we give up on ourselves" (xviii).

I have no intention of giving up on fancy. As long as I wield power over a course syllabus, I intend to insist that all my students read disturbing books.

7. METAPHORICAL THINKING IS A LIFE SKILL

Most students associate metaphorical thinking and symbolism only with their English classes. They are shocked when you tell them that they use metaphors every day. "Who, me? No way, Mrs. Jago. Only flakes and drips talk like that!"

"And what do you think I see when you say 'flake'? A snowflake? A flake of dandruff? Cornflakes?"

"No, you know what I mean, someone flakey, like Claire."

"Let's leave names out of it. What kind of a person are you referring to?"

"Well, someone with their head in the clouds. No sense. Can't remember things. Kinda screwy."

Everyday language is full of metaphors. Young people use them instinctively. I try to help them see what classical writers and poets do as a natural extension of their own creative use of images to portray an idea. One example that seems to bring this concept home (another metaphor) for students is the Apple, Inc., logo. Everyone is familiar with the cutout image of an apple with a bite taken from the corner. I ask students to consider why they think the computing company chose this image as its signature and what the symbol suggests.

The first response is often that the logo reminds them of A is for Apple in alphabet books and first-grade wall charts. I nod. "What else?" Another student will recall the apple from the Garden of Eden and Eve's famous bite. "But what does this have to do with computers?" Before long someone suggests that maybe Apple wants consumers to think that buying one of their machines will give people access to knowledge, like taking a bite of the fruit from the Tree of Knowledge. "What else?" (I always ask this even when I don't myself know what else could possibly be said.) Someone suggests that Apple probably wants their products to be seen as sexy and tempting, even a little bit dangerous. I nod again. "We've come up with two conflicting interpretations of this logo. Can they both be correct? Is it possible that Apple Computers wants us to see their products as both schoolroom wholesome and sexy?" All around the room they nod now.

I have no inside information about how Apple chose its name or logo. Maybe it was someone's favorite fruit. What I do know about is the power of symbols. Whatever conscious thinking went into the company's decision to use an apple, unconsciously they felt the image was just the right one to send it out into the world as a symbol of their work.

Metaphorical thinking is not just the province of poets and flakes. It is a life skill. By examining imagery, metaphor, and symbols in classical literature, students begin to understand how words work their magic on us. It is not just practice for an AP test, it is training for the real world. Persuasive speakers like Abraham Lincoln and Martin Luther King Jr. were masters of metaphor. One of the most effective images in King's "I Have a Dream" speech is that of a check. King began the extended metaphor by saying that "we have come to our nation's capital to cash a check" and goes on to compare America's treatment of blacks with a bounced check marked "insufficient funds." King refuses to believe that there is not enough capital in our country's "great vaults of opportunity" and so insists on presenting this check for payment "Now."

Again and again King conjured up concrete images to represent complex ideas helping his audience to envision what he wants to teach them. For example, in his plea for passive resistance, King says, "Let us not seek to satisfy our thirst for freedom by drinking from the cup of bitterness and hatred." Trying to help his listeners imagine a different world from the one they live in, he says, "With this faith we will be able to transform the jangling discords of our nation into a beautiful symphony of brotherhood." The power of Martin Luther King, Jr.'s language put the civil rights movement squarely on the national agenda.

Classical literature can also offer us the words we need when emotion leaves us tongue-tied. As our only child, James, boarded the plane to Tulane University for his first year of college, my husband and I found ourselves instinctively turning to *Hamlet*, reciting to him Polonius' speech to his son, Laertes, bound for France, "Aboard, aboard, for shame! The wind sits in the shoulder of your sail, / And you are stay'd for. There—my blessing with thee!" Of course, like the long-winded Polonius we couldn't leave it there but had to start giving James advice. "Look thou character. Give thy thoughts no tongue, / Nor any unproportion'd thought his act. / Be thou familiar, but by no means vulgar . . . Neither a borrower nor a lender be . . . / This above all—to thine own self be true, / And it must follow, as the night the day, / Thou canst not then be false to any man" (I.iii). Just like Laertes, James smiled, turned a deaf ear, and waved good-bye.

When cuts in the state budget compelled my school district to seek community support for a parcel tax, the Save Our Schools committee asked me to write a letter they might use in their publicity. I found myself instinctively resorting to metaphor.

> Think of a man asked to build a house. Imagine his only tool is a paintbrush. The man may manage to create a picture of a house, but this image will be two-dimensional, unable to support weight or offer shelter. So it will be for students and teachers. Without the proper tools: books, paper, desks, microscopes, calculators, computers, libraries, we can but create a poor picture of education. The doors may remain open and classes continue to meet, but learning will suffer.

Compelling metaphors can be persuasive. The more vivid the comparison, the more convincing the message.

No argument for the practical purposes of reading classical literature would be complete without reference to A. E. Housman's "Terence, This Is Stupid Stuff" (1987, 88). In the poem Housman defends depressing poetry. He suggests that it can serve as an antidote to the hard times that we all inevitably face one day, "Luck's a chance, but trouble's sure." Though some may find respite from troubles in beer and good times, the comfort to be found there is transitory. Terence—Housman's name for himself—recommends that we "train for ill and not for good" and promises to "friend you, if I may, / In the dark and cloudy day." The poem concludes with a parable about a king who, bit by bit, built up his immunity to venom (reminiscent of Rappachini's daughter, Beatrice) and thereby survived his rivals. Hausman argues that reading dark poetry can do the same for us and similarly save lives.

> Terence, this is stupid stuff:
> You eat your victuals fast enough;
> There can't be much amiss, 'tis clear,
> To see the rate you drink your beer.
> But oh, good Lord, the verse you make,

It gives a chap the belly-ache.
The cow, the old cow, she is dead;
It sleeps well the horned head:
We poor lads, 'tis our turn now
To hear such tunes as killed the cow.
Pretty friendship 'tis to rhyme
Your friends to death before their time
Moping melancholy mad:
Come, pipe a tune to dance to, lad.

Why if 'tis dancing you would be,
There's brisker pipes than poetry.
Say, for what were hop-yards meant,
Or why was Burton built on Trent?
Oh many a peer of England Brews
Livelier liquor than the Muse,
And malt does more than Milton can
To justify God's ways to man.
Ale, man, ale's the stuff to drink
For fellows whom it hurts to think:
Look into the pewter pot
To see the world as the world's not.
And faith, 'tis pleasant till 'tis past:
The mischief is that 'twill not last.
Oh I have been to Ludlow fair
And left my necktie God knows where,
And carried half-way home, or near,
Pints and quarts of Ludlow beer:
Then the world seemed none so bad,
And I myself a sterling lad;
And down in lovely muck I've lain,
Happy till I woke again.
Then I saw the morning sky:
Heigho, the tale was all a lie;
The world, it was the old world yet,
I was I, my things were wet,
And nothing now remained to do
But begin the game anew.

Therefore, since the world has still
Much good, but much less good than ill,

And while the sun and moon endure
Luck's a chance, but trouble's sure,
I'd face it as a wise man would,
And train for ill and not for good.
'tis true, the stuff I bring for sale
Is not so brisk a brew as ale:
Out of a stem that scored the hand
I wrung it in a weary land.
But take it: if the smack is sour,
The better for the embittered hour;
It should do good to heart and head
When your soul is in my soul's stead;
And I will friend you, if I may,
In the dark and cloudy day.

There was a king reigned in the East:
There, when kings will sit to feast,
They get their fill before they think
With poisoned meat and poisoned drink.
He gathered all that springs to birth
From the many-venomed earth;
First a little, thence to more,
He sampled all her killing store;
And easy, smiling, seasoned sound,
Sate the king when healths went round.
They put arsenic in his meat
And stared aghast to watch him eat;
They poured strychnine in his cup
And shook to see him drink it up:
They shook, they stared as white's their shirt:
Them it was their poison hurt.
—I tell the tale that I heard told.
Mithridates, he died old.

—*A. E. Housman*

Great literature has always helped me in an "embittered hour." I want students to have similar access to succor.

All About Words

Polonius: What do you read, my lord?
Hamlet: Words, words, words.

(*Hamlet,* II.ii)

MY ALL-TIME favorite worst opening to a student paper is "Every book is made up of words. In *Catcher in the Rye,* J. D. Salinger uses many words." Poor Danny was trying to follow the instructions a previous teacher had given him about opening an essay with a reference to the larger world. He fell into the trap of mistaking the obvious for insight.

Yet Danny put his finger on an important issue in literature study. One of the things that makes teaching classical literature difficult is all the pesky words. Every time I ask a group of teachers to examine the first pages of a classic and then ask them to describe the challenges this text poses for students, the first response is invariably "vocabulary." Why are our students' vocabularies so limited? Why don't kids know more words? The obvious answer is that they don't read enough. Keith Stanovich described the problem as the Matthew Effect, referring to the Gospel of Matthew, "Unto every one that hath shall be given, and he shall have abundance: but from him that hath not shall be taken away even that which he hath" (Matt. 25:29). Children who read build huge vocabularies from immersion in the world of language. They aren't consciously trying to learn new words; it just happens. Those for whom reading is a trial avoid books. As a result they learn many fewer words per day, per week, per year than their reading peers. By the time they are handed a copy of *Great Expectations* in ninth grade—to my mind an outstanding choice for freshmen full of great expectations in high school—many students are familiar with fewer than 80 percent of the words in Dickens' novel. Vocabulary experts tell us that for reasonable reading comprehension a student needs to know 90–95 percent of the words.

It would be so much tidier if there were a magic list we could have every student memorize and thereby immunize them against vocabulary problems for evermore. Learning language doesn't work that way. We can only reasonably teach about 300–400 words per year through direct instruction (Nagy, Anderson, and Herman 1987). What teachers can do is help students develop habits of mind for approaching unfamiliar vocabulary. Children making good progress as readers add between 3,000 and 5,000 new words to their vocabulary per year through incidental exposure. If students are doing so well on their own, why should teachers bother? The reason is that the children who are furthest behind in vocabulary development are also the ones adding the fewest words per year. Their rate of language acquisition is far lower than that of their reading peers. It is only through teachers' sustained attention to vocabulary development that these students will be able to make the progress they need. Learning 400 carefully targeted words can improve comprehension significantly.

Stahl and Shiel (1992) found that for vocabulary instruction to make a difference, it must be productive. That is, it must involve teaching a target set of words that generates knowledge of a much larger set of words. They recommend:

- teaching prefixes, suffixes, and roots;
- teaching students to derive meaning from context; and
- teaching words as part of semantic groupings.

VOCABULARY AND EDGAR ALLAN POE'S "THE FALL OF THE HOUSE OF USHER"

I try to combine all three methods. Given that my students cannot write in their books and circle interesting and unfamiliar vocabulary, I hand them bookmarks (see Figure 2.1) and ask them to list on the slip of paper four to five words from their homework reading with page numbers. At the beginning of class the next day I invite students to share words from their bookmarks and record them on chart paper. Edgar Allan Poe's short story "The Fall of the House of Usher" is an excellent text for this exercise. To remind you of the flavor of Poe's diction, here is his first paragraph.

> During the whole of a dull, dark, and soundless day in the autumn of the year, when the clouds hung oppressively low in the heavens, I had been passing alone, on horseback, through a singularly dreary tract of country; and at length found myself, as the shades of the evening drew on, within view of the melancholy House of Usher. I know not how it was—but, with the first glimpse of the building, a sense of insufferable gloom pervaded my spirit. I say insufferable; for the feeling was unrelieved by any of that half-pleasurable, because poetic, sentiment, with which the mind usually receives even the sternest natural images of the desolate or terrible. I looked upon the scene before me—upon the mere house, and the simple landscape features of the domain—upon the bleak walls—upon the vacant eye-like windows—upon a few rank sedges—and upon a few white trunks of decayed trees—with an utter depression of soul which I can compare

FIGURE 2.1   Vocabulary Bookmark

My personal vocabulary list	
Word	Page

Copy the bookmarks on card stock, possibly in a light color, but with no other distracting or cutesy features. Your intent on is to enrich, not to distract, from the reading. You know the prop is working when students ask you if they can please have a new one.

May be copied for classroom use. © 2004 by Carol Jago, from *Classics in the Classroom*. Portsmouth, NH: Heinemann.

to no earthly sensation more properly than to the after-dream of the reveller upon opium—the bitter lapse into everyday life—the hideous dropping off of the veil. There was an iciness, a sinking, a sickening of the heart—an unredeemed dreariness of thought which no goading of the imagination could torture into aught of the sublime. What was it—I paused to think—what was it that so unnerved me in the contemplation of the House of Usher? It was a mystery all insoluble; nor could I grapple with the shadowy fancies that crowded upon me as I pondered. I was forced to fall back upon the unsatisfactory conclusion, that while, beyond doubt, there are combinations of very simple natural objects which have the power of thus affecting us, still the analysis of this power lies among considerations beyond our depth. It was possible, I reflected, that a mere different arrangement of the particulars of the scene, of the details of the picture, would be sufficient to modify, or perhaps to annihilate its capacity for sorrowful impression; and, acting upon this idea, I reined my horse to the precipitous brink of a black and lurid tarn that lay in unruffled lustre by the dwelling, and gazed down—but with a shudder even more thrilling than before—upon the remodelled and inverted images of the gray sedge, and the ghastly tree-stems, and the vacant and eye-like windows. (1984, 317–18)

From their reading of the story my tenth graders offered the following words from their bookmarks:

entombment
cadaverously
phantasmagoric
gossamer
clangorous
miasma

As I wrote "entombment," I asked the student who proffered the word if there was any part he recognized. Before Jorge could answer, three others shouted out, "tomb!" Then I asked, "Do you know what the prefix *en-* does to a word? What about the suffix *-ment?*" Together we recalled that *en-* means "into" so *entomb* must mean putting someone into a tomb. As *-ment* means "state of" and turns a verb into a noun, *entombment* must mean being buried. We checked the dictionary (my students bought me an electronic pocket dictionary for my birthday after I admired one of theirs) and found that the definition for *entombment* was "the state of being placed in a grave." I model what readers do every time they meet a word they don't know. My Spanish-speaking students hold many clues to the meaning of English in the cognates they already know. I help them practice putting together the pieces.

Of course prefixes, suffixes, and roots will have limited use with a word like *miasma.* Since students copy the page number where they find the word, I could ask Jenny to read the sentence from the story where the word appeared. Jenny read, "These appearances, which bewilder you, are merely electrical phenomena not uncommon—or it may be that they have their ghastly origin in the rank miasma of the tarn." I had told them the day before that a *tarn* was a small body of water. I asked Jenny if she knew what *rank* meant. She said, "stinking" and I figured that was close enough. "What else can you guess about *miasma?* Do you think it's something pleasant or unpleasant? Can you find any clues in the sentence?"

Others in the class again interrupted. "It's *ghastly!* Maybe it's a ghost or ghostly."

"You're close. *Miasma* is a poisonous atmosphere that was thought to rise from swamps and putrid matter."

"Ugh! Gross. This is disgusting."

I ask students to look at our list of words again and to think about what feelings these words triggered. They said that the words gave them the creeps. Poe's choice of vocabulary had been successful. I wanted to demonstrate how Poe's diction helped create this mood so I asked students to choose a page—any page—in the story and to scan it for words that they felt helped to establish the eerie, melancholy mood. These didn't need to be unfamiliar words; they could be any words that they felt contributed to the "creepy" feeling they described. Luke's list looked like this:

Words that established the mood
gloom
intolerable
agitation
terror
hesitation
apathy
tremor
excavation

I had students share their lists with one another and then in small groups try to come to a consensus about how Poe's words contributed to the mood of the story. What could they conclude about his choice of words? Students—including those who had gotten very little from their individual reading of the story—spoke insightfully about the effect Poe's language had upon them. "It makes you feel like you're inside a nightmare." "I just kept seeing black. There's no color or light anywhere." "Really depressing." "This Poe guy needs help."

The key learning that I try to achieve is that learning new words is a natural act. So much of what happens in schools seems artificial to students, a series of meaningless assignments that they must perform for the teacher or else fail. Inviting students to bring their words to class and making these words the focus of instruction seems to help students buy into the work.

CRITERIA FOR CHOOSING WHICH WORDS TO TEACH

I mentioned in passing that I had explained the word *tarn* before asking students to read "The Fall of the House of Usher." Nouns like this (and *sedge* and *fissure)* can be huge stumbling blocks to comprehension and need to be addressed before students sink with Poe into a slough of despond. Most literature anthologies provide lists of words to pre-teach before reading a selection, but the criteria for choosing which words sometimes seems idiosyncratic. In *Bringing Words to Life* Isabel Beck, Margaret McKeown, and Linda Kucan urge teachers to consider the utility of words when deciding which words to teach. How important is this word to comprehension of the passage? How useful will this word be to students for future reading? They identify three central criteria:

- *Importance and utility:* Words that are characteristic of mature language users and appear frequently across a variety of domains
- *Instructional potential:* Words that can be used in a variety of ways so that students can build rich representations of them and of their connections to other words and concepts.
- *Conceptual understanding:* Words for which students understand the general concept but that provide precision and specificity in describing the concept. (2002, 19)

Their third criterion has implications for student writing as well as for reading comprehension. By examining the myriad words Edgar Allan Poe employs to create a nightmarish mood, students expand their own range of expression. Without words to make distinctions and to "provide precision and specificity" there is little clarity. Think of all the pedestrian student stories you have read over the years. "It was a dark and stormy night." Consider how much better these stories could be if students knew more words.

WHAT DOES IT MEAN TO "KNOW" A WORD?

I don't know about you, but I am very bad at defining words off the top of my head. When students contribute vocabulary words from their bookmarks for me to add to our class list, I almost always know the word but struggle to find the right phrase to explain what the word means. Watching me agonize may have inspired my students to proffer the pocket dictionary. The painful mental search has brought home to me the clear difference between having an idea about what a word means and being able to recall a definition. There are levels of understanding vocabulary. Good readers proceed with what they know about a word, adding to what they know with each new context and fresh encounter. Dale and O'Rourke (1986) describe four levels of "knowing" a word:

> Stage 1: Never saw it before.
> Stage 2: Heard it, but don't know what it means.
> Stage 3: Recognize it in context as something to do with . . .
> Stage 4: Know it.

I am constantly astounded by the number of words my high school students insist that they have never seen or heard, common words like *desolate, ponderous, emaciated.* Of course such vocabulary is only common in written text. The Matthew Effect strikes again. Those students who don't read find themselves drowning in Stage 1 words and therefore can't comprehend the text well enough to deepen their understanding of their Stage 2 and Stage 3 words. The paucity of vocabulary feeds on itself.

The solution is not to abandon the study of literature for all but a gifted few but to make reading literature rich in language and full of powerful, varied diction a part of every child's experience from kindergarten on. Even before students can negotiate texts as readers they can be initiating their own future relationship with words through teachers reading aloud. Let's look at the vocabulary in the first paragraph of Kenneth Grahame's *The Wind in the Willows,* a book that delights the youngest of children:

> The Mole had been working very hard all the morning, spring-cleaning his little home. First with brooms, then with dusters; then on ladders and steps and chairs, with a brush and a pail of white-wash; till he had dust in his throat and eyes, and splashes of white-wash all over his black fur, and an aching back and weary arms. Spring was moving in the air above and in the earth below and around him, penetrating even his dark and lowly little house with its spirit of divine discontent and longing. It was small wonder, then, that he suddenly flung down his brush on the floor, said 'bother!' and 'O blow!' and also 'Hang spring-cleaning!' and bolted out of the house without even waiting to put on his coat. Something up above was calling him imperiously, and he made for the steep little tunnel which answered in his case to the gravelled carriage-drive owned by animals whose residences are nearer to the sun and air. So he scraped and scratched and scrabbled and scrooged, and then he scrooged again and scrabbled and scratched and scraped, working busily with his little paws and muttering to himself, 'Up we go! Up we go!' till at last, pop! his snout came out into the sunlight, and he found himself rolling in the warm grass of a great meadow. (1983, 7)

This may be the first time children encounter the words *discontent, imperiously,* and *muttering* but, in the context of the story, the words communicate their meaning. A good teacher might draw their attention to these words and have students consider moments when they have felt discontented or heard someone muttering. Children could take turns giving directions to one another imperiously. Over time these words will move through the stages until students know them well. Whether or not they can pin a dictionary definition to the word is less important than developing the habits of mind for learning new words. According to eminent reading scholar Jeanne Chall (Chall and Jacobs 1996), students benefit from reading aloud through eighth grade.

"Knowing" a word involves more than the word's definition. It also means knowing how a word functions in different contexts. Students may be familiar with *bolted* in terms of a locked door but in Grahame's story *bolted* refers to how Mole dashes from his underground house. A full and flexible knowledge of a word includes an understanding of the breadth of a word's use. Children raised on books learn this without even trying. Given that so many of our students have not had this grounding in language, the urgency to help them learn words is tremendous. Some look at the language gap between high-performing students and low-performing students and give up hope. I say school is our only hope. Watching situation comedies and reality programs on television won't increase their vocabulary. Neither will conversations with peers. To accelerate the rate at which students are learning new words they need daily exposure to quality literature combined with strategic instruction.

EFFECTIVE VERSUS INEFFECTIVE VOCABULARY INSTRUCTION

What does this strategic instruction entail for middle and high school students?

Do	Don't
• Choose literature for your curriculum that is rich in vocabulary. • Make word study an integral part of every day's lesson. • Use personalized examples when defining new words. "I wonder if Wendy's *doleful* expression is a result of not having her homework completed." • Keep lists of new words posted around your classroom for constant reference. Try to use these words as you teach. • Create tasks for students that make them pay attention to words they don't know. • Model how you use prefixes, suffixes, and roots to help you figure out a word's meaning. • Model how you use context to help you figure out a word's meaning. • Encourage students to try out the new words they are learning in their writing. Reward their efforts. • Celebrate questions about words. Never be afraid to say, "I don't know. Let's check the dictionary." The best vocabulary teacher is a person who loves learning new words.	• Have students look up lists of words in the dictionary and copy out definitions. • Ask students to use these defined words in "meaning-laden" sentences without classroom discussion of the word's multiple meanings and use. • Administer vocabulary quizzes that punish students who may be learning many new words yet earn a D or F because all the words on the list began as complete unknowns (Stage 1 words). • Hand out word searches or other word games and puzzles that eat up valuable instructional time that is needed for reading, talking, and writing. • Give students a full period to illustrate one word. This isn't an art class. Fifty-five minutes to learn one word isn't a good enough return (even if these posters do look great hung around the room).

Words for Talking About *Julius Caesar*

Students need to develop their vocabulary for a variety of reasons, not simply to be able to read words on the page. They also need words to express what they think and feel about literature. For many students the subtlety of their thinking is compromised by the paucity of their language. I have found that rich literature can serve as a springboard for building vocabulary. Take, for example, William Shakespeare's *Julius Caesar*. Despite the play's title, the central character is Brutus, a Roman senator. The sooner students can grasp this character, the more comprehensible the action of the play will be. If they don't understand Brutus, all you have is tedium in togas. To help students begin I open our study of the play with four words:

Key words	Definitions
honorable	deserving or winning honor and respect
gullible	easily deceived or duped
stoic	one who is seemingly indifferent to or unaffected by joy, grief, pleasure, or pain
idealist	one whose conduct is influenced by ideals that often conflict with practical considerations

As we read Act I, scene ii, I ask students to see if they can find evidence of any of these traits in Brutus.

BRUTUS: What means this shouting? I do fear the people
Choose Caesar for their king.

CASSIUS: Ay, do you fear it?
Then must I think you would not have it so.

BRUTUS: I would not, Cassius; yet I love him well.
But wherefore do you hold me here so long?
What is it that you would impart to me?
If it be aught toward the general good,
Set honour in one eye and death i' th' other,
And I will look on both indifferently;
For let the gods so speed me as I love

The name of honour more than I fear death.

CASSIUS: I know that virtue to be in you, Brutus,

As well as I do know your outward favour.

Well, honour is the subject of my story.

I cannot tell what you and other men

Think of this life; but for my single self,

I had as lief not be as live to be

In awe of such a thing as myself.

I was born free as Caesar; so were you.

We both have fed as well, and we can both

Endure the winter's cold as well as he.

For once, upon a raw and gusty day,

The troubled Tiber chafing with her shores,

Caesar said to me, 'Dar'st thou, Cassius, now

Leap in with me into this angry flood

And swim to yonder point?' Upon the word,

Accoutred as I was, I plunged in

And bade him follow. So indeed he did.

The torrent roar'd, and we did buffet it

With lusty sinews, throwing it aside

And stemming it with hearts of controversy.

But ere we could arrive the point propos'd,

Caesar cried, 'Help me, Cassius, or I sink!'

I, as Aeneas, our great ancestor,

Did from the flames of Troy upon his shoulder

The old Anchises bear, so from the waves of Tiber

Did I the tired Caesar. And this man

Is now become a god, and Cassius is

A wretched creature and must bend his body

If Caesar carelessly but nod on him.

He had a fever when he was in Spain,

And when the fit was on him, I did mark

How he did shake. 'Tis true, this god did shake.
His coward lips did from their color fly,
And that same eye whose bend doth awe the world
Did lose his lustre. I did hear him groan.
Ay, and that tongue of his that bade the Romans
Mark him and write his speeches in their books,
Alas, it cried, 'Give me some drink, Titinius,'
As a sick girl! Ye gods, it doth amaze me
A man of such a feeble temper should
So get the start of the majestic world
And bear the palm alone.

Shout. Flourish

BRUTUS: Another general shout?
I do believe that these applauses are
For some new honours that are heap'd on Caesar.

CASSIUS: Why, man, he doth bestride the narrow world
Like a Colossus, and we petty men
Walk under his huge legs and peep about
To find ourselves dishonourable graves.
Men at some time are masters of their fates.
The fault, dear Brutus, is not in our stars,
But in ourselves, that we are underlings.
'Brutus,' and 'Caesar.' What should be in that 'Caesar'?
Why should that name be sounded more than yours?
Write them together: yours is as fair a name.
Sound them: it doth become the mouth as well.
Weigh them: it is as heavy. Conjure with 'em:
'Brutus' will start a spirit as soon as 'Caesar.'
Now in the names of all the gods at once,
Upon what meat doth this our Caesar feed
That he is grown so great? Age, thou art sham'd!
Rome, thou hast lost the breed of noble bloods!

When went there by an age since the great Flood
But it was fam'd with more than with one man?
When could they say (till now) that talk'd of Rome
That her wide walls encompass'd but one man?
Now is it Rome indeed, and room enough,
When there is in it but one only man!
O, you and I have heard our fathers say,
There was a Brutus once that would have brook'd
Th' eternal devil to keep his state in Rome
As easily as a king.

BRUTUS: That you do love me I am nothing jealous.
What you would work me to, I have some aim.
How I have thought of this, and of these times,
I shall recount hereafter. For this present,
I would not (so with love I might entreat you)
Be any further mov'd. What you have said
I will consider; what you have to say
I will with patience hear, and find a time
Both meet to hear and answer such high things.
Till then, my noble friend, chew upon this:
Brutus had rather be a villager
Than to repute himself a son of Rome
Under these hard conditions as this time
Is like to lay upon us.

CASSIUS: I am glad
That my weak words have struck but this much show
of fire from Brutus.

I ask students what evidence they found in this passage to support the claim that Brutus is

- an ***honorable*** man: Brutus puts other people before himself—"the general good" and cares more about honor than his own life.
- a ***gullible*** man: Brutus seems to fall for Cassius' faulty logic—just because someone is a poor swimmer or gets sick doesn't mean they shouldn't rule Rome. He may also have been swayed by Cassius' flattery with the comparison Brutus' name with Caesar's. (You should point out the similarity between this and the "rose by any other name" passage in *Romeo and Juliet.*)
- a ***stoic***: Brutus seems very calm compared with Cassius. At the end he doesn't become impassioned but simply says he has been thinking about these things and will think some more. (Further evidence for Brutus' stoicism appears later in the play.)
- an ***idealist***: Brutus says he would rather be a villager— unlikely to happen—than a senator under the current oppressive conditions in Rome. (As with his stoicism, further evidence of Brutus' idealism emerges as Cassius' practical plan for the murder of Caesar develops.)

I then ask students to choose one of these four words and to write for seven to eight minutes describing someone they know who is honorable, gullible, stoic, or idealistic. I urge them to include concrete examples of this person in action so that we can see why they think this is a defining character trait. After they write, I have students share what they have written with a partner. Once everyone has read to a partner, I ask if anyone has heard about an honorable character we all should know. When someone volunteers his or her partner, that person reads to the whole class. A gullible character? A stoic? An idealist?

As a final activity before assigning the rest of Act I for homework, I ask students to rate themselves in terms of these character traits. Where on a spectrum from most to least would they place themselves?

Most honorable————————————————Least honorable

Most gullible————————————————Least gullible

Most stoic————————————————Least stoic

Most idealistic————————————————Least idealistic

By the end of class we have not only established a strong basis for building an understanding of Brutus as a tragic hero but also learned and applied four powerful words, words that we will continue to employ throughout our study of the play.

3

Choosing Which Books to Teach

THE MOST IMPORTANT decision English teachers make in terms of curriculum is choosing which books to teach. Sometimes the decision is made for us by the availability of textbooks. Institutionalized titles—if it's tenth grade it must be *Julius Caesar,* if it's eleventh grade it must be *The Great Gatsby*—are hard to change. Individual teachers can influence the established order, but to do so you will need to base your choices on more than whim. As many young teachers have learned, "I loved *The Mayor of Casterbridge* so my students are sure to" can be a recipe for disaster. The more carefully thought-out your rationale for choosing a particular novel, the more convincing you will be as you offer the book to students. The clearer you are in your own mind about why Mary Shelley's *Frankenstein* is an important book for sixteen-year-olds, the more likely you will have the stamina to pull students through the opening epistolary section so that they can reach the heart of the matter.

Certain titles have become institutionalized in middle and high school English programs. This is clearly demonstrated by Arthur Applebee (1989) in his analysis of the most frequently required texts in grades 7 12:

1. *Romeo and Juliet*
2. *Macbeth*
3. *Huckleberry Finn*
4. *To Kill a Mockingbird*
5. *Julius Caesar*
6. *The Pearl*
7. *The Scarlet Letter*
8. *Of Mice and Men*
9. *Lord of the Flies*
10. *Diary of a Young Girl*
11. *Hamlet*
12. *The Great Gatsby*

Applebee's research revealed minimal changes to what has commonly been taught over the past twenty-five years. This need not be cause for lamentation. I argue that students should be reading and teachers need to be assigning about twice as many books as they currently do. With more titles in the curriculum, there is room for greater diversity. Increased reading will also produce a more literate populace.

In *Why Read the Classics?* (1999) Italo Calvino offers fourteen definitions of a classic:

1. The classics are those books about which you usually hear people saying: "I'm rereading . . ." never "I'm reading . . ."
2. The classics are those books that constitute a treasured experience for anyone who has read and loved them; but

they remain just as rich an experience for those who wait to read them until they can enjoy them.

3. The classics are books that exercise a particular influence, both when they imprint themselves on our imagination as unforgettable, and when they hide in the layers of memory disguised as the individual's or the collective unconscious.

4. A classic is a book that with each rereading, offers as much of a sense of discovery as in the first reading.

5. A classic is a book that even when we read it for the first time, gives the sense of rereading something we have read before.

6. A classic is a book that has never exhausted all it has to say to its readers.

7. The classics are those books that come to us bearing the aura of previous interpretations, and leaving behind them the traces of the culture or cultures (or just the languages and customs) through which they have passed.

8. A classic is a work that constantly generates a pulviscular cloud of critical discourse around it, but that always shakes the particles off.

9. Classics are books that, the more we think we know them through hearsay, the more original, unexpected, and innovative we find them when we actually read them.

10. A classic is the term given to any book that comes to represent the whole universe, a book on a par with ancient talismans.

11. "Your" classic is a book to which you cannot remain indifferent, and that helps you define yourself in relation or even in opposition to it.

12. A classic is a work that comes before other classics; but those who have read other classics first immediately recognize its place in the genealogy of classic works.

13. A classic is a work that can relegate the noise of the present to a background hum.

14. A classic is a work that persists as background noise even when a totally incompatible present holds sway. (3–9)

WHEN MORE IS BETTER

In my yearlong tenth-grade class we read the following books in class. These works fall squarely inside Vgotsky's Zone of Proximal Development; my students would not be able to read these texts without the help of a teacher.

Fall Semester
The Odyssey, Homer
Beowulf
Grendel, John Gardner
Frankenstein, Mary Shelley
Julius Caesar, William Shakespeare

Spring Semester
Much Ado About Nothing, William Shakespeare
Cyrano de Bergerac, Edmund Rostand
The Woman Warrior, Maxine Hong Kingston
Points of View, James Moffett (short stories)
Eye of the Heart, Barbara Howe (Latin American short stories)
Reading Poetry, Robert DiYanni

Outside class students must read five books per semester. I do not offer students free choice but instead give them a list of twelve novels I believe educated teenagers should have read. Students read one book every three to four weeks and then meet in literature circles with other students who have read the same book. They write an analytical essay on each novel exploring characterization, themes, or setting. Sometimes I have students write in response to a prompt. I often look at the AP Literature's open-ended questions for ideas. For my tenth graders, the texts listed fall within Vgotsky's Zone of Proximal Development. Students are able to read them with the help of their peers. Students choose one book from the short list below.

Fall Semester
A Lesson Before Dying, Ernest Gaines
All Quiet on the Western Front, Eric Maria Remarque
My Antonia, Willa Cather
The Catcher in the Rye, J. D. Salinger
The Bell Jar, Sylvia Plath
The Picture of Dorian Gray, Oscar Wilde
Brave New World, Aldous Huxley
Childhood's End, Arthur C. Clarke
Wuthering Heights, Emily Brontë
Black Boy, Richard Wright
The Stranger, Albert Camus
Bless Me, Ultima, Rudolfo Anaya

Students write literary term papers in the spring semester. Inevitably, many students choose authors they read in the course of the first semester. This year, in a class of thirty-six students, two chose Ernest Gaines; two, Sylvia Plath; one, J.D. Salinger; and one, Aldous Huxley. This is the first year in a long time that no one wrote a term paper on Albert Camus. This suggests to me that the books they read at my direction spurred them to want to read more of these authors and want to

A Note on Writing About Literature

The California English Language Arts Standards require students to write analytical essays in response to literature from fourth through twelfth grades. Students are tested on this skill through a direct writing assessment at fourth, seventh, and tenth grades. I almost always assign essays about literature based on the books students read outside class rather than those we study together. My rationale is that by the time we work our way through a novel or play, most of the themes and characters have been explored. Students' papers would merely be parroting back what we talked about in class. By having them write about books they read outside of class, there is more room for developing their interpretive skills. Students meet in literature circles to discuss these books, so they are not working in isolation. The literature circle groups do double duty as peer editing groups when students are ready to revise.

know more about how these authors work. Once their research is completed and the papers are turned in, students choose from lists arranged by theme or subject for outside reading. Students choose one book from each list.

Man's Intolerance to Man

Kaffir Boy, Mark Mathabane
Night and *Dawn,* Elie Wiesel
Maus I and *II,* Art Spiegelman
Imagining Argentina, Lawrence Thornton
One Day of Life, Manlio Argueta
Black Like Me, John Howard Griffin

Contemporary Women's Literature

The Women of Brewster Place, Gloria Naylor

Obasan, Joy Kogawa

The Poisonwood Bible, Barbara Kingsolver

The Handmaid's Tale, Margaret Atwood

The Joy Luck Club, Amy Tan

Jasmine, Bharati Mukerjee

My sophomore students read a total of twenty books. Do students struggle to keep up? Of course they do! We are not working in the Zone of Minimal Effort. Are there years when I fall behind and have to cut a title? It happens. California's standardized testing program significantly cuts into instructional time. Does the occasional student resort to Cliffs Notes or SparkNotes when he or she falls behind in the reading? I have no doubt about it. Knowing this does not reduce my expectations, however. I require a lot from students, and by and large they live up to these expectations.

I ask students to keep a log of all the books they read over the course of the year inside their portfolios. I would like to institutionalize at our school a procedure that the English department at Mira Costa High School in California has had in place for years—a four-year record of their reading. Seniors could examine their lists and write a reflective essay on the role that reading plays in their lives making reference to individual books. Figure 3.1 is a sample of the form I hope my department will adopt. One of the reasons I find this idea so compelling is that I would love to have seen my own list of books read from those years. Call it a cultural artifact.

There is no categorical imperative to use the selected books I list here. I am always on the lookout for compelling novels that encourage thinking about big ideas. I also try to teach one new work every year so that the repertoire of books I know well continues to grow.

FIGURE 3.1   Keeping Track of Reading

9th grade		10th grade		11th grade		12th grade	
Title	Date	Title	Date	Title	Date	Title	Date

CRITERIA FOR CHOOSING BOOKS

There is an art to choosing books for students. First I look for literary merit. Without this, the novel will not stand up to close scrutiny or be worth the investment of classroom time. Many good books that students love to read and should read do not belong on a course syllabus. Texts that work best for whole-class study

- are written in language that is perfectly suited to the author's purpose;
- expose readers to complex human dilemmas;
- include compelling, disconcerting characters;
- explore universal themes that combine different periods and cultures;
- challenge readers to reexamine their beliefs; and
- tell a good story with places for laughing and places for crying.

Great literature deepens our experience, heightens our sensibilities, and matures our judgment. I believe that teenagers want to have these experiences but have not realized that reading books can provide them. Warner Berthoff explains that literature "bears witness to significant human action, and to the possibility of such action, by re-creating concentrated versions of it within some discernible field of occurrence; to bear witness, that is, to what in specific acts of thought and feeling men and women . . . actually do and undergo in life" (1986, 7–8). Though students may complain that nobody looks anything like Beowulf anymore, it was not by accident that the headline of most newspapers on May 2, 2003, "Bush Hails Victory in Iraq," was accompanied by a photo of President George W. Bush emerging from a helicopter wearing a flight suit. Conquering heroes glory in their gear.

Beowulf returned to Hrothgar's hall in chain mail with Grendel's head on a stick and waving the hilt of his magic sword. The ghost of Hamlet's father appears to him in full battle dress. Poor, indecisive Hamlet worries that he will never be the man his father was. As literature teachers, it is our challenge to help students see the archetypal connections between the world they live in and the world of myth.

While the length of a book is not an important criterion, it is interesting to note that many of the classics most commonly taught fall in the two hundred-page range: *Of Mice and Men, 1984, Animal Farm, The Pearl, The Old Man and the Sea, The Red Badge of Courage.* Instead of eliminating longer works from the curriculum, teachers need to figure out ways to help students persist and prevail. I am forthright with my students about the fact that they are going to have to give up some of their TV and telephone time in order to complete their reading. Students have the time for longer books. They just need to be persuaded to reallocate minutes from other pleasures.

It is often our unfamiliarity with texts other than those on Applebee's list that keeps us teaching the same books year after year. I am fortunate to have been an addicted reader since childhood and so have read a great many books—albeit with varying degrees of understanding. I remember reading *The Scarlet Letter* in sixth grade before the facts of life had been explained to me. I didn't know what Hester Pryne's *A* stood for or what adultery involved, yet I liked the story and was proud to be carrying around such a complex book. I worry when some of my youthful colleagues who have never read the classics with any pleasure argue for their elimination on the grounds that students hate them. Could it be that these teachers don't understand the books well enough to make them accessible to kids? Deep knowledge about the literature—understanding the historical setting, the author's background, the impact the text had on readers in its own time, the peculiarities of the author's style, the work's structure—is essential for classroom success.

A Note on Recommended Readings from the Massachusetts English Language Arts Curriculum Framework

All students should be familiar with American authors and illustrators of the present and those who established their reputations after the end of World War II, as well as important writers from around the world, both historical and contemporary. During the last half of the twentieth century, the publishing industry in the United States devoted increasing resources to children's and young adult literature created by writers and illustrators from a variety of backgrounds. Many newer anthologies and textbooks offer excellent selections of contemporary and world literature.

As they choose works for class reading or suggest books for independent reading, teachers should ensure that their students are both engaged and appropriately challenged by their selections. The lists following are organized by grade clusters PreK–2, 3–4, 5–8, and 9–12, but these divisions are far from rigid, particularly for the elementary and middle grades. Many contemporary authors write stories, poetry, and nonfiction for very young children, for those in the middle grades, and for adults as well. As children become independent readers, they often are eager and ready to read authors that may be listed at a higher level. As suggested earlier in the Reading and Literature Strand of this framework, teachers and librarians need to be good matchmakers, capable of getting the right books into a child's hands at the right time.

The lists are provided as a starting point; they are necessarily incomplete, because excellent new writers appear every year. As all English teachers know, some authors have written many works, not all of which are of equally high quality. We expect teachers to use their literary judgment in selecting any particular work. It is hoped that teachers will find here many authors with whose works they are

(continues)

already familiar, and will be introduced to yet others.

Massachusetts English Language Arts Curriculum Framework, June 2001.

A copy of Massachusetts' lists can be found at *www.doe.mass.edu/frameworks/current.html*

The huge investment of preparation time required to teach a new novel also keeps us teaching the same texts. Helpful as packaged lesson plans and teacher materials on the Internet may be, I have to put in at least twenty hours of study before I am ready to teach a work for the first time. When I decided to teach Faulkner's *The Sound and the Fury,* I spent most of my spring break reading, rereading, and thinking about the Compson family. It is not simply a matter of generating new handouts or creating a day-by-day plan (which I did but revised almost as soon as I began using it) but, rather, a deep knowledge of the book itself that I needed to acquire. In an ideal world a teacher should have enough preparation time to be able to reread what she has assigned students every night before class. We know how difficult this is to accomplish when you meet 150-plus students a day and have their papers to read as well. Even so, I know that I am a better teacher on those days when I have made the time to reread.

To encourage investment in our own preparation, teachers should be allowed to become experts at a specific grade level. Often the vagaries of a school's master schedule cause teachers to oscillate between grades and therefore across texts with the result that they never develop deep knowledge of particular works. It is only when I have taught a complex work like *Hamlet* or *Invisible Man* at least twice that I feel that I begin to do justice to the book and, thus, to my students.

READING FOR EMPATHY

Many law and medical schools have begun to require their students to take courses in literature. Directors of these programs have found that knowledge of science and the constitution do not provide the full background necessary for optimal performance in the field. Effective attorneys and doctors need to understand human needs and emotions. They must learn about the human heart. For this knowledge one must turn to stories. At Columbia University medical students are assigned Leo Tolstoy's "The Death of Ivan Ilych." Ivan Ilych is a judge who falls incurably ill in middle age. Smug and selfish, Ilych's sickness isolates him further. Death appears to him as a continuation of the years that have gone before.

> From that moment the screaming began that continued for three days, and was so terrible that one could not hear it through two closed doors without horror. At the moment he answered his wife he realized that he was lost, that there was no return, that the end had come, the very end, and his doubts were still unsolved and remained doubts. (1960, 154)

Only Ilych's servant Gerasim is able to afford him relief. He does this by lifting his legs and offering simple words of comfort. Only in death does Ilych begin to live and reach out to someone, to something beyond himself.

Dr. Rita Charon, a humanities professor at Columbia University's medical school, has done research into what she calls "narrative medicine." She has found that the study of literature sharpens a medical student's ability to empathize with patients as well as to diagnose. Good doctors know how to listen to a patient's story and make sense of details and tone. Good readers do this. Literature allows for close, almost scientific analysis of individuals under duress. Anyone working with abused children could learn as much from Toni Morrison's *The Bluest Eye* or Keri Hume's *The Bone People* as they would from any clinical text.

The same is true in the study of law. Richard Wright's *Native Son* should be required reading for anyone contemplating work in the justice system. It is the story of Bigger Thomas, a young black man who in a moment of panic murders and then decapitates a wealthy white woman. His attorney's plea for mercy in sentencing lays out the moral dilemma Bigger poses for society:

> I ask that you spare this boy, send him to prison for life. . . . You cannot kill this man, Your Honor, for we have made it plain that we do not recognize that he lives! So I say, "Give him life!" This will not solve the problem which this crime exemplifies. That remains, perhaps, for the future. But if we say that we must kill him, then let us have the courage and honesty to say: "Let us kill them all. They are not human. There's no room for them." Then let us do it. We cannot, by giving him life in prison, help the others. We do not ask that this Court even try. But we can remember that whether this boy lives or dies, the marked-off ghettoes where this boy lived will remain. The mounting tide of hate on the one hand, and guilt on the other, one engendering fear and hate and the other engendering guilt and rage, will continue to grow. (1979, 404–5)

Set in Chicago in the 1930s, *Native Son* is as relevant and necessary to any discussion of social justice today as it was on the day it was written.

Now let us consider our students, many of them estranged from the adults in their lives. Their influences come primarily from popular culture and the media. How are these young people to develop empathy for others, to know individuals unlike themselves, to walk in someone else's shoes except through literature? Just as future doctors and lawyers need to read stories about suffering and injustice, so do our students. Some might agree in principle but then argue that students can learn these same lessons from more accessible books. Walter Dean Myers', *Monster* is one example that might be offered. While I think *Monster*—another story of a black boy on trial—is an excellent book and lobbied for its inclusion on our district's eighth-grade summer reading list, I do not believe it is of the caliber high school teachers should be choosing for classroom study. Students don't need a teacher's help to understand *Monster*. Most will gobble it up in two hours. *Native Son* does not go down so easily. At 430 pages, Wright's novel requires ten to twelve hours of intense reading and poses huge questions at every turn. Without a teacher's guiding hand, many young readers won't persevere. Without the excitement of classroom conversations about how the murder seems to free Bigger or how killing his girlfriend, Bessie, was different from killing the white girl, students may lose their way in this complex tale.

When students wail, "But what does this have to do with me?" I can only reply, "Everything. Everything!" They just don't know it yet.

CHOOSING TO TEACH MARY SHELLEY'S *FRANKENSTEIN*

Why would any high school English teacher choose Mary Shelley's *Frankenstein*? The text is dense, the language obscure, the plot unrealistic, and the conclusion tragic. A teacher who wants students to love literature might resist selecting such a novel. But Shelley's work is truly "novel." Let's examine how *Frankenstein* measures up to the criteria established earlier in this chapter.

Frankenstein Is Written in Language That Is Perfectly Suited to Mary Shelley's Purpose

> It was on a dreary night of November that I beheld the accomplishment of my toils. With an anxiety that almost amounted to agony, I collected the instruments of life around me, that I might infuse a spark of being into the lifeless thing that lay at my feet. It was already one in the morning; the rain pattered dismally against the panes, and my candle was nearly burnt out, when, by the glimmer of the half-extinguished light, I saw the dull yellow eye of the creature open; it breathed hard, and a convulsive motion agitated its limbs. (1988, 48)

Frankenstein is a gothic novel, a genre popular during the time Mary Shelley penned this story. Such novels are full of mystery, horror, and the supernatural and are often set in wild and remote places. The action commonly takes place in haunted castles and revolves around inexplicable events. The language in this opening paragraph of Chapter 5 is typical of this genre. It is not by accident that Mary Shelley has the monster come to life on a stormy winter night. The light has almost gone out around Victor Frankenstein when the metaphorical light of life awakens the creature. Notice how the final weighty sentence builds to a climax. Mary Shelley tells us the time, 1 A.M., a time when ordinary men are abed. Then we hear the sound of rain on the windows. The single candle has almost gone out when the narrator sees his creation come to life. The monster opens an eye, breathes, and makes his first movement. The author appeals to our senses to see, hear, and feel the terror that Victor feels on that dreary November night when he played at being God. The long, cumulative sentence makes readers hold their breath in fear and awe.

Mary Shelley's choice of words contributes to the brooding atmosphere: *dreary, beheld, toils, anxiety, agony, infuse.* I like taking a paragraph like this one and asking students to identify which words contribute most to its mood. I want students to see that while authors may choose words instinctively the words are also intentional and artful selections. To demonstrate this I ask students to insert the following words in their place and see how even when the meaning remains the same, the mood is destroyed.

dreary—dull
beheld—saw
toils—work
anxiety—worry
agony—pain
infuse—pour

It was on a *dull* night of November that I *saw* the accomplishment of my *work.* With a *worry* that almost amounted to *pain,* I collected the instruments of life around me, that I might *pour* a spark of being into the lifeless thing that lay at my feet.

Together with her artful use of syntax and diction, Mary Shelley is a master of gothic imagery. The pictures she creates in a reader's mind are entirely consistent with her assumed narrative purpose: "a dreary night of November," "instruments of life," "spark of being," "lifeless thing," "rain pattered dismally," "half-extinguished light," "dull yellow eye," and "convulsive motion." Making students aware of Shelley's use of syntax, diction, and imagery can help persuade struggling readers that she didn't employ these writer's tools to make life more difficult for readers but rather to enhance the impact of her story.

Frankenstein Exposes Readers to Complex Human Dilemmas

The early 1800s were a time of startling breakthroughs in science and technology. In Mary Shelley's introduction to her novel (written fifteen years later) she describes the scientific talk that swirled around her. These were new and dangerous ideas.

> Many and long were the conversations between Lord Byron and Shelley to which I was a devout but nearly silent listener. During one of these, various philosophical doctrines were discussed, and among others the nature of the principle of life, and whether there was any probability of its ever being discovered and communicated. They talked of the experiments of Dr. Darwin (I speak not of what the doctor really did or said that he did, but, as more to my purpose, of what was then spoken of as having been done by him), who preserved a piece of vermicelli in a glass case till by some extraordinary means it began to move with voluntary motion. Not thus, after all, would life be given. Perhaps a corpse would be reanimated; galvanism had given token of such things; perhaps the component parts of a creature might be manufactured, brought together, and endued with vital warmth. (1988, xvi)

Shelley goes on to describe how this late-night conversation inspired a dream, a nightmare in which she saw "the pale student of unhallowed arts kneeling beside the thing he had put together." From the story's inception, Shelley knew that she would explore the terror Victor Frankenstein felt at his success, "he would rush away from his odious handiwork, horror-striken." This complex human dilemma—scientific achievement overreaching man's ability to use new-found knowledge wisely—is the heart of the novel.

Frankenstein Includes Compelling, Disconcerting Characters

Victor Frankenstein's unnamed creation is one of literature's most compelling and disconcerting characters. He is also a character who has stepped out of Mary Shelley's book and into popular culture. Almost everyone has heard of Frankenstein although many think "Frankenstein" is the monster rather than the creator's name. Filmmakers have made the image of an eight-foot Boris Karloff lurching through the wild with bolts in his neck a ubiquitous image, a Halloween favorite. The real monster is actually a more interesting character. While he may not be much to look at, Shelley's creature is educated, even erudite. He is articulate and desires human contact. He does not have the brain of a criminal, though abuse and depression cause the creature to resort to murder. Can abandonment of a laboratory experiment be considered child abuse? How would you feel if you knew that your mother fainted dead away at her first sight of you?

Frankenstein Explores Universal Themes That Combine Different Time Periods and Cultures

Northrop Fry defines a classic as a work that refuses to go away. *Frankenstein* explores the timeless theme of man's dangerous fascination with creation. Although the book is a work of its own time, a time when scientists were first beginning to experiment with the potential of science to improve human life, the book serves as a cautionary tale for all time. Newspaper editorials on cloning or genetic engineering often make reference to *Frankenstein*. Arguing for ethical constraints, writers cite the disastrous effects of Frankenstein's experiment as supporting evidence. In a *Los Angeles Times* commentary titled "Keep Us Human: If We're Truly Smart, We'll Refuse to Foolishly Tamper with our DNA," Bill McKibben warns of the dangers of genetic engineering even for such obvious benefits as prolonging life. The impetus for Victor Frankenstein's experiment was his mother's untimely death. McKibben concludes his essay by saying, "A species smart enough to discover the double helix should be wise enough to leave it more or less alone" (April 14, 2003). This message will resonate for students who know how the brilliant but foolish Victor Frankenstein brought destruction to his entire family through misguided experimentation.

I always conclude our study of *Frankenstein* with a day spent reading articles on genetic engineering and discussing the dangers of scientific discovery run amok. Online newspaper archives now make finding such editorials and printing them out for students a simple matter. This subject always seems to incite passionate arguments both for and against experimentation, and I choose it for that reason. The lesson demonstrates the universal nature of Mary Shelley's themes. I make sure that students don't leave class without being reminded of this. Such days are the best of times.

Frankenstein Challenges Readers to Reexamine Their Beliefs

Many young people are naïve optimists regarding the potential of science to improve human life. *Frankenstein* challenges them to consider the unintended consequences of playing [at being] God in the laboratory. For those interested in reading a contemporary novel depicting a society destroyed by genetic engineering I recommend Margaret Atwood's *Oryx and Crake.* In this science fiction tale a scientist creates a "perfect" species of humans with the DNA to survive in a world that humans have destroyed. It is not a pretty picture. Atwood has the uncanny ability to take bits of what is already scientifically possible and spin a tale that terrifies readers. Even the most adamant proponents of scientific experimentation are forced to consider the implications of research fueled by greed and gain rather than by ethical principles.

Frankenstein Tells a Good Story with Places for Laughing and Places for Crying

I must concede that according to this criterion Mary Shelley's novel lets you down a bit. There are not many places for laughing in *Frankenstein,* but on the whole it tells a darned good story. True to its gothic nature, the story's brooding atmosphere and tragic conclusion causes readers to feel pity—and shed a few tears—both for Victor Frankenstein and for his ill-begotten creation.

If a book cannot measure up to these criteria, it will probably not serve you well as a classroom text. In an essay called "What's So Great About Great Books," Dinesh D'Souza (2003) writes, "It is less important for students to learn *about* the great books than it is for them to learn *from* the great books" (56). I don't teach the classics out of arrogance or simply to give students what D'Souza calls "cocktail party familiarity with a canon of great works." I teach them because they raise and urge students to examine fundamental human questions. With our time in literature courses so limited—fifty-five minutes a day times fewer than 180 days a year when you take into consideration pep assemblies, standardized testing, visits from counselors, and emergency drills—to choose otherwise seems folly. Selecting literature for your class isn't a matter of finding books that students like. It's about teaching stories that make them think.

4

How Stories Work

MOST OF MY students pick up an assigned book expecting not to understand it. Their experience in English classes has taught them that if they just sit back and wait, the teacher will stop asking questions and ultimately explain what it all means. If they are lucky, this is all she will ask about on the test. Students are also convinced that authors deliberately make literature difficult. When the story isn't immediately accessible, they turn away complaining, "It's boring!" Instead of yielding to student complaints and moving into that Zone of Minimal Effort, I try to teach students how to navigate difficult text. I believe it is our job not simply to drag students through a series of books but rather to show them how stories work. By succeeding in this endeavor, we help students acquire power over text.

THE ELEMENTS OF LITERATURE

The elements of literature provide readers with the tools they need for navigating stories. Plot and structure, character, setting, point of view, style and language, symbol, and theme are the building blocks of fiction. They work together to convey meaning. When students tell me that they hate a story, what they sometimes are really saying is that they don't understand what they read. I try to help them suspend judgment until they see how the elements of the piece converge. Researchers Beck and McKeown (1981) found that when students map these elements and then identify them either as they read or upon reflection, comprehension improves dramatically.

Literary elements provide an organizing framework for understanding a story.

- "Who?" leads readers to characters
- "Where?" and "When?" to setting
- "What?" "Why?" and "How?" to plot
- "So what?" to the author's purpose and theme

Readers need answers to these questions in order to plot their position in a story. I will be the first to admit that a great deal of bad teaching has focused on filling in the blanks on worksheets or answering—in complete sentences, please—simplistic questions about literary elements. I can remember as a student being in awe of my teachers' ability to identify themes. How did teachers do this? What did they know that I didn't? It seemed a magical skill. As a teacher I try to dispel all illusion of magic and make my own process of thinking about a story transparent. I want students to see that identifying literary elements can serve as guideposts to understanding. Massachusetts literature standard LS12 for grade 8 reads, "Students will identify, analyze, and apply knowledge of the structure and elements of fiction and provide evidence from the text to support their understanding" (Massachusetts Department of Education 1997).

For easy reference, here is a list of the most commonly referred-to elements of fiction. Sven Birkerts, author of *The Gutenberg Elegies: The Fate of Reading in an Electronic Age* (1994), compares these various elements to the ingredients of a sauce, all essential, though some more essential than others.

Character.   A character is an individual in a work of fiction. Though characters always possess human traits, they need not always be human. Rounded characters are dynamic and lifelike. Flat characters are static and often stereotypical.

Plot.   The plot is the story line. It is important to distinguish between plot and narrative that is a simple retelling of events. E. M. Forster did this most elegantly when he explained that while "The king died and the queen died" is a narrative, "The king died, and the queen died of grief" is a plot. With the inclusion of "grief," we suddenly have the suggestion of cause and effect between the two events. The plot of a story entails the relationships and connections between events.

Setting.   The setting is the physical location and time period in which a story occurs. The setting situates a reader in time and place. Often one builds an impression of the setting from a series of scattered details—a sea breeze, the ships on the horizon, the grasses underfoot, harbor etiquette. Time and place create a context for the story.

Theme.   The theme consists of an insight about human nature that the writer communicates through the story. Themes are often elusive and are rarely stated directly. They are woven deeply into the fabric of the work. A rich piece of literature may contain several themes.

Point of View. The vantage point from which a story is told is the point of view. The most commonly used points of view are first person, third person limited, and omniscient narration. Second-person narration does occur in literature (see Carlos Fuentes' novella *Aura* or Jay McInerney's *Bright Lights, Big City*), but it creates problems for the writer with a story to tell. When the point of view is first person one of the characters tells the story using "I." The reader can know only what this narrator knows and reports. When the point of view is third person limited, the story is told from the point of view of a character in the story. The omniscient narrator is the most widely used vantage point in fiction. The story is told from the point of view of a neutral narrator, more like a camera than a character. In many cases this narrative point of view is presumed to be the author's.

Tone. The writer's attitude toward the work is called the tone. Sven Birkerts describes tone as "*how* the *what* gets told." To determine the tone of a story a reader must consider the nature of the voice doing the telling. Is the voice ironic? Is it nervous or excited? Is it calm and detached or wary and suspicious? What kind of language is being used? Casual, everyday words or formal, elevated language? There is a close relationship between the tone of a story and the point of view from which it is told.

THE ELEMENTS OF JACK LONDON'S *THE CALL OF THE WILD*

Jack London's *The Call of the Wild,* like most of his works, deals with the elemental struggle for survival—a subject all young people, even those from the center of the biggest cities, can relate to. He wrote in a naturalistic style, presenting the harsh realities of the world without moral judgment. *The Call of the Wild* is the story of a sled dog, Buck, during the time of the Alaskan gold rush. Kidnapped from his comfortable home and

exposed to the arctic wilderness, Buck finds that his primitive instincts
are awakened. Buck serves his various Alaskan masters dutifully, even
those who abuse him. When John Thornton rescues Buck from a group
of incompetent miners, Buck learns about loyalty and love. With John's
death, Buck answers the call of the wild, severing his connection to
humanity and joining his brother wolves.

One of the most interesting elements of this novel is its point of
view. Told in the third person, the tale is Buck's story. Readers can only
see, hear, or know what Buck sees, hears, and knows. This differs from
a first-person point of view in that the story is not told in Buck's voice.
No doubt the fact that Buck is a dog influenced London's choice here.
One effect of this use of the third person singular is that it allowed
London to demonstrate the folly of humans when seen through the eyes
of an outside observer, in this case an intelligent dog.

Buck is the protagonist in this novel. He is the character who
changes throughout the course of the story and with whom the reader
sympathizes. Buck does not progress in the same way a human character might primarily because his goal is different. Most human protago-
nists move toward established norms in society or toward
achievement—either material or spiritual. Buck moves away from society and back to the wild. "The call of the wild" is a metaphor for Buck's
desire to leave the world of human folly and return to the wolves. Taken
literally, the call is the wolves crying at night. Symbolically this call rep-
resents the call inside Buck's blood and his longing for freedom in the
wild. Though he had found a deep connection with a human through
John Thornton, Buck was tired of being a pet. London also explores the
irony that the dignity and virtue Buck exhibits even under duress should
be so lacking in many of the story's human characters.

In Chapter 7 London writes,

One night he sprang from sleep with a start, eager-eyed, nostrils quiv-
ering and scenting, his mane bristling in recurrent waves. From the

forest came the call (or one note of it, for the call was many-noted), distinct and definite as never before—a long-drawn howl, like, yet unlike, any noise made by husky dog. And he knew it, in the old familiar way, as a sound heard before. (1981, 126)

Character, setting, point of view, theme, and tone all interact to create a powerful impression.

Difficult, challenging texts like *The Call of the Wild* offer young readers insight into the wider world than the one they inhabit. When teachers determine that the novel's setting is too foreign or that the point of view is too confusing, we shortchange students. They may not be able to read this book without your help, but with critical attention to the elements of literature, students can enter London's fictional world. This will require them to move outside their Zone of Minimal Effort, but if you offer the scaffolding, most will thank you for making them work.

STORY STRUCTURES

Authors also draw from a stock of familiar narrative structures. During the 1970s, David Rumelhart organized the insights of cognitive researchers into a comprehensive grammar for narrative text. For experienced readers these patterns form an arc they know well. A hero or heroine takes center stage. Trouble emerges. Help appears, sometimes from an unlikely source. Complications develop. Things get worse and worse until the conflict is finally resolved. Freytag's Pyramid is a graphic organizer commonly used to describe a story's structure. This mapping of the classic pattern of fiction and drama charts the key structures of the story: exposition, rising action, climax, falling action, and denouement or resolution.

I use Freytag's Pyramid (Figure 4.1) in several different ways. Sometimes I chart the course of events on a large poster prominently displayed as we read. This seems particularly helpful for Shakespeare plays. Students who are absent can easily see where today's reading fits within the whole. At other times I ask students to draw the triangle and then to map the events of the work using Freytag's model. This method works best just as students have completed a text and before we begin any of the culminating activities. It sometimes helps to have students include page numbers with events. I like having students do this in small groups rather than individually. When we post the various groups' pyramids, students are intrigued to see how other groups have chosen to represent the structure of the story.

In "Remembrance of Things Parsed: Story Structure of and Recall," Mandler and Johnson (1977) expanded Rumelhart's theory of a story grammar to include a study of the events taking place within the story. They examined and built into their ideas about story grammar the hero's goals, the path taken, failed and successful attempts to solve the problem, ultimate outcomes. They explored questions such as, "When all was said and done, what did the main character feel? What had he or she learned?" In Chapter 6 I demonstrate how this structure can be used to describe Odysseus' journey.

Research by Pressley (Pressley, et al. 1989) suggests that stories that conform to story grammar structure are easier for students to read

FIGURE 4.1   FREYTAG'S PYRAMID

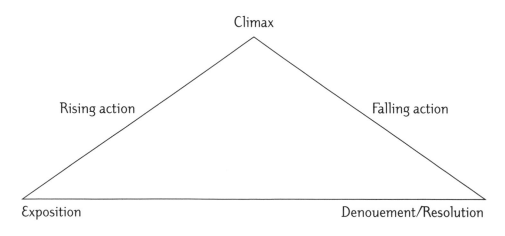

and remember than stories that take alternate forms. Charting the course of the story can help students see how what they are reading, unfamiliar as the characters and setting may at first seem, actually conforms to a pattern they know well. Stories that withstand the test of time stimulate readers both by confirming our expectations and at the same time surprising us. Gifted authors and storytellers work within a framework. They use familiar literary elements. At the same time, they always seem to find a way to say something new.

Recent research from cognitive science indicates that students remember what they think about. (I know this seems too obvious to need saying, but I'm always delighted when science confirms what I observe every day.) What immediately struck me as I read Daniel T. Willingham's article in the summer 2003 issue of *American Educator* were the implications of his research for literature teachers. If "what ends up in a learner's memory is not simply the material presented—it is the product of what the learner thought about when he or she encountered the material" (37), then books that demand hard thinking on the part of a reader are more likely to be remembered than those students breeze through. Effort imprints the reading on students' minds. I want Victor Frankenstein, Beowulf, Odysseus, Brutus, and Cyrano to live in my students' memories forever. Thinking through these characters' complex stories, figuring out how the stories work, should help this to happen.

LITERARY DEVICES

Most students consider the formal study of literary devices the epitome of school for school's sake. They contend that nobody apart from the occasional English teacher cares a jot about figures of speech. What they don't understand is that understanding how literary devices work gives readers power over text. The more clearly students understand how a writer works his magic in a line of poetry or prose, the better able they will be to analyze that line. Some might argue that such analysis can only happen in honors or Advanced Placement classes, but I believe that all students can and should be shown how language works.

In *Literature as Exploration,* Louise Rosenblatt asserts that "The problem that the teacher faces first of all, then, is the creation of a situation favorable to a vital experience of literature. Unfortunately, many of the practices and much of the tone of literature teaching have precisely the opposite effect" (1983, 61). Remembering how we had been taught literature in high school with heavy emphasis on form and background over any kind of authentic reader response, many of us embraced Rosenblatt's theories with open arms. We stopped teaching students about literary devices and focused on eliciting authentic readers' responses. We banished any reference to literary terminology from our lessons. In retrospect, I think this was a mistake. I also don't think for a minute that this was what Louise Rosenblatt intended.

The language of literature helps readers express what we see in what we read. Terms like *personification, alliteration,* and *metaphor* give us words to describe what we see and feel as we read. Knowing these terms makes students more articulate. None of this is to suggest that we turn our conversations about literature into games of literary trivial pursuit: find the simile, identify the alliteration, spot the allusion. I teach the specialized vocabulary of literature study in order to facilitate richer discussion. Mastering this vocabulary has also helped to make the transition to Advanced Placement courses and college English classes much less stressful. You won't need to quiz students on these definitions if you simply use the terms on pages 69–71 regularly. I keep a running list of words posted in my classroom that we refer to each time I employ a literary term as I teach. Seeing the words daily helps students accept them as the natural language of literature study.

Alliteration: the repetition of initial consonant sounds

Allusion: a reference to another work with which the author expects the reader to be acquainted

Antagonist: a character opposed to the protagonist

Apostrophe: a figure of speech in which a character or force is addressed directly

Archetype: a prototype upon which later characters, images, stories, or themes are modeled

Blank verse: unrhymed verse, frequently in iambic pentameter, imitative of human speech

Climax: the turning point or point of maximum tension in a story

Conceit: an extended metaphor

Connotation: the suggestion or implication of a word or expression; though *house* and *home* have the same denotation as a place of shelter, the two words have very different connotations

Denotation: the explicit meaning of a word, the dictionary definition

Denouement: the resolution of a story, a French term referring to the untying of knotted threads

Diction: a writer's word choice

Dynamic character: a rounded character, who changes over the course of the story

Exposition: the first stages of a story where the author provides information necessary to understand subsequent events

Falling action: the part of the story that follows the climax and is commonly full of trouble for the hero

Figurative Language: language used in suggestive rather than literal ways; figurative language in poetry includes simile, metaphor, and personification

Flat characters: characters that don't change over the course of the story and are typically used as background figures

Foreshadowing: hints and suggestions that offer readers clues to future developments in a story

Hyperbole: intentional overstatement

Imagery: verbal pictures or other sensory detail

Irony: the tension that arises from the discrepancy, either between what one says and what one means (verbal irony) or between what a character believes and what a reader knows (dramatic irony)

Metaphor: a figure of speech that makes a direct comparison without the use of the words "like" or "as"

Narrative Poem: a story in verse

Onomatopoeia: the use of words whose sound or pronunciation implies their meaning

Personification: a figure of speech in which abstract ideas, inanimate objects, or animals are given human characteristics

Prose poem: a form of prose characterized by rhythmic patterns and figurative language similar to that of poetry

Protagonist: the main character or hero/heroine of a story

Refrain: a sentence or phrase of one line or more repeated in a poem, often at the end of a stanza or between stanzas

Rhyme: repetition of sound in accented syllables that appear in similar positions within lines of poetry

Rhythm: the regular recurrence and speed of sound and stresses in a poem or work of prose—writers use rhythm to intensify the meaning of words, slowing it when the effect is reflective and hastening it to portray excitement

Rising action: the events that lead up to and cause the climax of a story, often called "complications"

> **Simile:** a figure of speech that makes a comparison between two objects using "like" or "as"
>
> **Symbol:** a thing, person, or event used to represent a larger idea
>
> **Theme:** the central meaning or idea of a literary work
>
> **Tone:** the attitude expressed by the style and overall presentation and reflected mainly through syntax and diction
>
> **Understatement:** intentional declaration that less is the case, the opposite of hyperbole

The very best handbook of literary terms that I have ever used is M. H. Abrams' *A Glossary of Literary Terms.* Now in its seventh edition, the volume is a collection of short essays on the terms used in literature. While it is expensive and often difficult to locate in bookstores, you will want this book for your professional library. Just take care when you lend it to see that it is returned.

THE ELEMENTS OF JOHN STEINBECK'S *THE GRAPES OF WRATH*

At Santa Monica High School tenth-grade students who intend to enroll in eleventh-grade Advanced Placement Language and Composition are required to read *The Grapes of Wrath* over the summer. Like many other schools across the nation, our eleventh-grade English honors course attempts to cover both the traditional American literature curriculum and the AP language and composition curriculum. In order to help students begin this considerable undertaking—and to help them decide whether they should take up the challenge of advanced placement work—I offer them the following sampling from the end of Chapter 25. One of the reasons the novel works so well as an introduction to English 11AP is that the text is both a historically important fictional work and a series of richly crafted essays about the plight of the dispossessed. This interchapter provides a rich sampling of Steinbeck's style and an introduction to many of *The Grapes of Wrath*'s important themes. In order to maintain scarcity and high prices, the California produce growers are destroying their produce. All around them Dust Bowl refugees are starving.

> The little farmers watched debt creep up on them like the tide. They sprayed the trees and sold no crop, they pruned and grafted and could not pick the crop. And the men of knowledge have worked, have considered, and the fruit is rotting on the ground, and the decaying mash in the wine vats is poisoning the air. And taste the wine—no grape flavor at all, just sulfur and tannic acid and alcohol.
>
> This little orchard will be part of a great holding next year, for the debt will have choked the owner.
>
> This vineyard will belong to the bank. Only the great owners can survive, for they own the canneries too. And four pears peeled and cut in half, cooked and canned, still cost fifteen cents. And the canned pears do not spoil. They will last for years.
>
> The decay spreads over the State, and the sweet smell is a great sorrow on the land. Men who can graft the trees and make the seed fertile and big can find no way to let the hungry people eat their produce. Men who have created new fruits in the world cannot create a system whereby their fruits may be eaten. And the failure hangs over the State like a great sorrow.
>
> And the smell of rot fills the country. . . . In the souls of the people the grapes of wrath are filling and growing heavy, growing heavy for the vintage. (1999, 348-49)

After we read the passage, I ask students to find examples of powerful metaphors and imagery, copy these onto a chart like the one in Figure 4.2, and consider what effect these images have on their understanding of Steinbeck's message. I always remind students to unpack a simile by stating the qualities of the familiar object being compared, for example the nature of tides. Once they have worked on their charts for about fifteen minutes, I ask them to share what they have written with a partner. Students are always surprised to see how others have interpreted the images they chose. I then ask if they noticed any literary devices in the passage.

- How did the similes, sensory images, and personification contribute to the overall effect of the passage?
- Why do you think Steinbeck chose to employ these devices?
- How did they contribute to your understanding of the passage?

Though there is much that students do not understand about this excerpt—remember this is their first taste of the book—they come away from the lesson with a sense of what kind of story this is going to be.

Graphic organizers are artificial structures designed to help students look more closely at text. Every time I use one I tinker with the headings or rearrange the columns on the page. Instead of making blank copies for students, I draw one sample form on the board and have them draw it themselves. My goal is not to achieve a set of perfectly filled-in forms but to instill an understanding of the elements of literature.

FIGURE 4.2   Steinbeck Metaphors

Steinbeck's images and metaphors	What they make me feel and think	What they suggest about Steinbeck's message
"The little farmers watched debt creep up on them like the tide"	This line makes it seem as though the farmers are drowning. Little people drown more easily than big people so little farmers are probably more vulnerable than big farmers.	Tide comes in slowly . . . but it always comes. This might be suggesting that the little farmers didn't realize what was happening to them at first but now they are under water in terms of debt and can't survive. Comparing their situation to the tide might also have something to do with the inevitability of all this happening. Kinda depressing. Not much hope here.
"the debt will have choked the owner"	It sounds as though the debt is alive and dangerous. Like an evil force. I see someone strangling the farmer.	Steinbeck seems to be saying that the small farmers can't survive. They have been "choked."
"the sweet smell is a great sorrow"	This really gets me. I don't usually think of sweet smells as sorrowful but at a funeral the flowers sometimes make you sick with their smell. Also rotting fruit smells disgusting.	Maybe that's it. Steinbeck is saying that it's a funeral in California for all but the big landowners.

5

How Poems Work

STUDENTS NEED POETRY. Few recognize this need, and in fact many are outspoken in their hatred for the genre. These same teenagers spend hours every day listening to song lyrics in search of language that reflects their feelings. They know how particular rhythms make the heart pound while others soothe jangled nerves. They carry in their heads hundreds of memorized lines repeating them half-aloud to carry them through the day.

One method for helping students recognize the poetry all around them is to include familiar song lyrics and hip hop refrains in our classroom lessons. Much of the pleasure students take from contemporary music is a result of lyricists' conforming—whether songwriters or students realize it or not—to tried-and-true literary devices: rhyme, rhythm, alliteration, simile, metaphor, onomatopoeia, figurative language, hyperbole, understatement.

In her book *Rules for the Dance,* poet Mary Oliver attempts to explain why it is important for students to experience poetry.

> Poems speak of the mortal condition; in poems we muse about the tragic and glorious issues of our fragile and brief lives: our passions, our dreams, our failures. Our wonderings about heaven and hell—these too are in poems. Life, death, mystery, and meaning. Five hundred years and more of such labor, such choice thought within choice expression, lies within the realm of metrical poetry. Without I, one is uneducated, and one is mentally poor. (1998, xi)

Most of the students I teach have had minimal experience with close readings of poems, particularly of pre-twentieth-century poetry. I begin the study of poetry with the assumption that students will love these rich texts, and that it is my good fortune to be able to introduce them to giants like William Wordsworth. Every teenager needs to consider how "The World Is Too Much With Us."

LITERARY TERMINOLOGY AND "THE WORLD IS TOO MUCH WITH US" BY WILLIAM WORDSWORTH

Beginning the year with the study of poetry allows a teacher to introduce or—one hopes—reintroduce many literary terms that you will be using throughout the year. We want this terminology to become our common classroom language. Rather than handing students a list of terms to memorize, I ask the class to develop their own list. As I use the terms in discussing poems, students copy words and definitions into their notes. The simple act of putting down definitions in their own hand helps to make these terms more their own.

A Word on Literary Terminology

For many students the study of literary terminology is the epitome of school for school's sake. "Why do we need these made-up words, Mrs. Jago?" I answer that, just like physics and calculus, the study of literature has its own vocabulary. Words like *hyperbole, allusion,* and *connotation* help us be more articulate about what we see as we read. The more students use these words in class, the more natural it becomes to employ them in writing.

Posted in my classroom is a word wall of literary terms. The first time I use a term, I add it to the list. Each time I repeat it, I point to the word on the list and then embed the definition into my sentence. "How would you describe the tone of this poem? You know tone is the author's attitude toward the subject. What do you think Wordsworth thinks or feels about nature?" Like water dripping onto earth, the definitions become part of students' working vocabulary.

No need for nasty quizzes when students use the language of literature every day.

A teacher could take an entire class period offering students background information on Wordsworth's poem. You might talk about the Romatic Period and the genesis of lyrical ballads. You could also tell students about Wordsworth's love of the Lake District and the criticism he was receiving from conservative reviewers who called him an enemy of progress. The problem is that young readers don't have a place to store this information until they have made some sense of the text for themselves. Even if you have the classroom management skills to make a group of teenagers sit quietly and take notes while you lecture, their eyes quickly glaze over. I almost always start with the poem.

In *Six Walks in a Fictional Woods,* Umberto Eco has written, "il testo è una macchina pigra che necessita di essere attivata" ("The text is a lazy machine that needs to be activated," from U. Eco, Lector in fabula, Milano 1979). I tell students that poems are lazy machines. In order to turn the machine on they are going to have to do more than simply say, "I don't get it" and wait for a teacher to explain. In order to make sense of a poem, a reader needs to set that machine in motion. "Thinking aloud" is one strategy that helps.

Thinking Aloud

The goal is to make visible the thinking that goes on inside a good reader's head during a first reading. I try to make this invisible process transparent by reading the first few lines aloud to students with my internal commentary. I then have students work with partners, taking turns reading and thinking aloud about the poem. Good readers commonly

- pose questions,
- identify unfamiliar vocabulary or allusions,
- make connections to their own experience,
- rephrase inverted lines, and
- comment on the poem.

It helps to remind students that, as there will be many people talking at once, it will help to lower their voices. In some classes you may need to assign particular pairs to ensure that students work productively.

My modeled commentary is the italicized lines of the poem that follow. Of course, as someone who has read the Wordsworth poem many times before, you are re-creating an imagined first time through a text. You might want to have students bring in a contemporary poem to stump you with and use a think-aloud strategy in front of them cold. You want to demonstrate that on a first pass through a poem, one always has more questions than answers but that as one works through one's questions thoughtfully, carefully, with the help of a dictionary and sometimes of other readers, comprehension emerges. As Walt Whitman explained, "The process of reading is not a half-sleep; but in the highest sense an exercise, a gymnastic struggle; that the reader is to do something for himself."

The World Is Too Much With Us

The world is too much with us; late and soon,
Getting and spending, we lay waste our powers:
Little we see in Nature that is ours;
We have given our hearts away, a sordid boon!
This Sea that bares her bosom to the moon:
The winds that will be howling at all hours,
And are up-gathered now like sleeping flowers;
For this, for every thing, we are out of tune;
It moves us not.—Great God! I'd rather be
A Pagan suckled in a creed outworn;
So might I, standing on this pleasant lea,
Have glimpses that would make me less forlorn;
Have sight of Proteus rising from the sea;
Or hear old Triton blow his wreathèd horn.

William Wordsworth

The world is too much with us; late and soon,
I like the sound of this. Reminds me of my cell phone going off when I'm trying to think. I wonder why he says "late and soon" instead of sooner or later. Maybe it's for rhyme.
Getting and spending, we lay waste our powers:
Can't spend money unless you get it. I guess laying waste our powers means something like using up all your energy.
Little we see in Nature that is ours;
This line seems turned inside out, inverted. If I start the line with "We see" it makes simpler sense.

After pairs wrestle with the poem for ten minutes or so, I bring the class together and ask if there are unresolved questions. It is always more effective to respond to student questions—after checking that no one else in the classroom has answers—than simply offering information unbidden.

This think-aloud strategy has other benefits as well.

- It starts everyone in the class talking. The discourse in any literature class can easily become dominated by a few students. These few always seem to suck up all the oxygen in the room. The think-aloud activity requires everyone to speak.
- Students discover that they are not the only ones with questions or who find a line difficult to unpack.
- Students often express insights that surprise their partners, opening up the poem to richer interpretations.
- The intimacy of pairs invites personal reflection of a sort that might feel inappropriate or uncomfortable within the larger forum.

The first time you ask students to think aloud, be sure to take a moment to ask them what they feel they learned from the exercise. I want students to understand that they are employing a valuable comprehension strategy. We are practicing out loud what they will learn to do inside their heads.

Too often teachers make the mistake of stopping once they have elicited a personal response. I believe this is only the beginning. After this think-aloud activity, which should only take about ten to fifteen minutes of class time, I ask students to read the poem again to themselves and then to write for seven to ten minutes on what they think this poem is about.

I ask students to freewrite before we begin discussion of a text because it allows me to call on any student in the class without having it be a "Gotcha!" moment. Everyone has had a chance to think about the

---

A Word on Freewriting

This kind of response to literature has often been misused and misunderstood. Freewriting is a thinking exercise. Students take the ideas that emerge from their conversation with a partner and use writing to sort out their thoughts. The act of casting ideas into coherent sentences helps shape these ideas and pushes students to develop their thinking without fear of error.

I encourage students to use this time to express questions they have about the text. The articulation of a question often leads to tentative, exploratory answers. "Maybe Wordsworth is thinking . . ." "I wonder if . . ." Almost instinctively, students begin to interpret the poem.

This is not prewriting for an essay. Unless students need the threat of points to keep them on task, I wouldn't even collect their papers. I don't want to suggest by word or deed that this is kind of writing is a negotiable product.

Wordsworth poem and everyone has something to share. Some may have only questions, but the magic is that these are their questions, not mine.

When studying poems like this you may need to help students with words and phrases that are no longer common to our language. I commonly need to provide the following information in response to student questions about this poem:

- **"sordid boon"**: a shabby or somehow foul reward. The choice of these words suggests that Wordsworth views trading our relationship with nature for a lifetime of commerce as a bad bargain.

- **"suckled in a creed outworn"**: nurtured in an outdated/obsolete religion
- **lea**: meadow
- **Protcus**: is a sea god from Greek mythology. He is able to change shape at will. Some students may remember from *The Odyssey* that Odysseus had to wrestle Proteus for information about getting home to Ithaca.
- **Triton**: another sea god who serves Poseidon from Greek mythology. His special role is blowing a conch that controls the waves, the "wreathèd horn."

BACKGROUND KNOWLEDGE AND ALLUSIONS

Student questions about Proteus and Triton provide an opportunity to teach about *allusion.* Adding the term to our word wall of literary terminology, I tell students that allusions are references to something from history, religion, mythology, or literature. I invite them to bring in copies of literary allusions they find in the newspaper. Our display of allusions in the news grows quickly.

Examples of Allusion
- "Something Rotund in the State of Denmark"—an article on overeating in Scandinavia
- "Harvard? The Horror, the Horror!"—an article on competition in Harvard Law School
- "The Crime of Punishment Taints All of America"—an editorial on prison reform
- "Protesters Quietly Decry Frankenfood"—a news story about a march against farm technology and genetically altered food
- "It's Always 1984 in Cuba"—an opinion piece objecting to

the Supreme Court decision requiring public libraries receiving federal aid for Internet technology to install pornography
filtering software

- "Crime and Provenance: A Chosen Son Is Exiled"—a Sunday
Styles article on a young man accused of stealing art from
his former employer

I want students to see that the more familiar they are with classical literature, the more they will understand in the world around them. Some
students argue that the world of the *New York Times'* Sunday Styles isn't
their world, but I respond that whatever world they choose, knowledge
is power and ignorance always a handicap.

THE SONNET

One reason students don't have the skills to negotiate classical poetry is
that we hadn't taught them how poems work. In our urgency to abandon
the lecture format, literature teachers may have adopted too passive a role.
We want to continue to make genuine student response the cornerstone
of the classroom, but withholding information about how poems work
may make it impossible for some students to have any response at all.

One has only to consider Quincy Troupe's poem on Magic
Johnson to see that truly "novel" poems continue to be written. Yet
poets employ a common set of building blocks, both in terms of form—
sonnet, haiku, villanelle, and ballad—as well as in terms of literary
devices. When Quincy Troupe spoke at my high school, he emphasized
the importance of wide reading for anyone who hoped to write. "How
can you create something new if you don't know what's been done?"
Responding to a question from the audience about what else an aspir-
ing poet should do besides read, Troupe advised the young man to

begin by mastering the traditional forms. "Free verse can wait. Learn your craft."

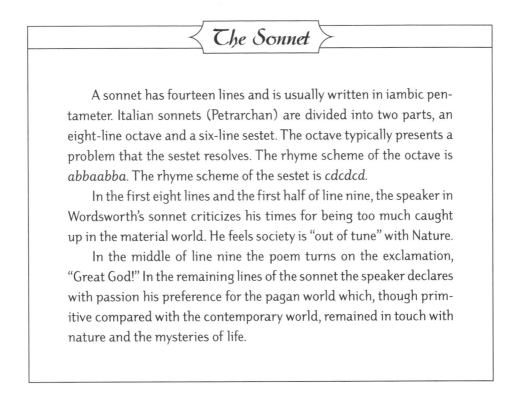

A sonnet has fourteen lines and is usually written in iambic pentameter. Italian sonnets (Petrarchan) are divided into two parts, an eight-line octave and a six-line sestet. The octave typically presents a problem that the sestet resolves. The rhyme scheme of the octave is *abbaabba*. The rhyme scheme of the sestet is *cdcdcd*.

In the first eight lines and the first half of line nine, the speaker in Wordsworth's sonnet criticizes his times for being too much caught up in the material world. He feels society is "out of tune" with Nature.

In the middle of line nine the poem turns on the exclamation, "Great God!" In the remaining lines of the sonnet the speaker declares with passion his preference for the pagan world which, though primitive compared with the contemporary world, remained in touch with nature and the mysteries of life.

I always ask students to consider why William Wordsworth would choose a traditional structure like the sonnet for a poem advocating a return to more primitive times. Nikki responded, "Maybe he wanted to prove that he knew all these rules. I mean, somebody reading a poem by a guy who says he'd rather be a pagan might think Wordsworth was some kind of barbarian. But to do all this rhyming stuff you have got to be educated. I think Wordsworth used a sonnet to get readers to take him seriously." Nikki's response demonstrates how alert she is to the ways form reflects the author's purpose.

Poems like "The World Is Too Much With Us" continue to be read because they offer insight into the human condition, insight that is not bound by the temporal conditions which inspired its creation. I am always looking for questions to trigger the leap from past to present. Questions like:

- Do you find that electronic devices like cell phones cause the world to be too much with you?
- Is a return to more primitive ways a practical solution?
- Do you think it is possible to remain in tune with Nature and yet "get and spend"?

Another way to help students see that the sonnet is not an archaic form is to read contemporary sonnets. U.S. Poet Laureate Billy Collins has written a delightfully irreverent poem called "Sonnet" that begins "All we need is fourteen lines, well, thirteen now, / And after this next one just a dozen." Collins goes on to poke gentle fun at the form all the while adhering to its structure. Edgar Allan Poe also wrote a tongue-in-cheek sonnet about writing sonnets. The "dear name" concealed within "An Enigma" can be found by reading the first letter of the first line, the second letter of the second line, the third letter of the third line to the end of the sonnet. Sarah Anna Lewis was a poet and friend of Poe. Explaining the hidden pattern to students and having them figure out the woman's name reinforces the sonnet's fourteen-line rule in their minds.

An Enigma

"Seldom we find," says Solomon Don Dunce,
"Half an idea in the profoundest sonnet.
Through all the flimsy things we see at once
As easily as through a Naples bonnet—
Trash of all trash?—how *can* a lady don it?
Yet heavier far than your Petrarchan stuff—

Owl-downy nonsense that the faintest puff
Twirls into trunk-paper while you con it."
And, veritable, Sol is right enough.
The general tuckermanities are arrant
Bubbles—ephemeral and *so* transparent—
But *this* is, now,—you may depend on it—
Stable, opaque, immortal—all by dint
Of the dear names that lie concealed within't.

Edgar Allan Poe

Once students have a handle on how sonnets work, you might ask them what they would expect from a poem titled "Sonnet Reversed." What might Rupert Brooke be saying about his subject by deciding to write his sonnet this way?

SONNET REVERSED

Hand trembling towards hand; the amazing lights
Of heart and eye. They stood on supreme heights.

Ah, the delirious weeks of honeymoon!
  Soon they returned, and, after strange adventures,
Settled at Balham by the end of June.
  Their money was in Can. Pacs. B. Debentures,
And in Antofagastas. Still he went
  Cityward daily; still she did abide
At home. And both were really quite content
  With work and social pleasures. Then they died.
They left three children (besides George, who drank):
  The eldest Jane, who married Mr. Bell,
William, the head-clerk in the County Bank,
  And Henry, a stock-broker, doing well.

Rupert Brooke

What is the effect of *beginning* the sonnet with a rhyming couplet? How is the final line, "And Henry, a stock-broker, doing well," a commentary on the couple's life?

Ninth-grade teachers at my school often integrate a unit on the sonnet within their study of *Romeo and Juliet.* A colleague of mine at Santa
Monica High School who teaches ninth grade, Meredith Louria, asks her
students to write their own sonnets and then publishes them in a booklet.
The slim volume holds a place of pride in our library. My favorites from
this year's collection are by Alice Ollstein and Sarah Orgel.

SONNET: A DAY WITHOUT

A day without your words is like a fast
For heart and soul can feel great hunger too.
A food-free day, a day without repast
Would seem a breeze compared to lack of you.
To live without your smile is to live
Much like a blind man stumbling in the night
With no bright torch, whose purpose is to give
One joy, your smile is my only light.
A day without your kiss is like a drought
When your sweet raindrops can't caress my lips.
My heart runs dry when I must do without
Those shivers sent from head to fingertips.
I do not need to eat or drink or see
For I have you; you are all of this to me.

Alice Ollstein

IT'S A "WONDER"

Beyond just dough, but not quite a pastry
Warm, chewy bread can always draw my smile
White, wheat, or grain, it is all so tasty
The sweet aroma can't help but beguile.
It is the start to a perfect repast
Butter, honey, or jam makes the right spread
Which I like best is which I had last
I say skip the meal, let's just eat the bread.

Yet it can be destroyed with little force
In a few minutes it can be burnt

Crumbly or stale the softness turns to coarse
Not quite the same when wet is what I've learnt.

But if stale or crumbly is all that's there
Please point me at it and just tell me where.

Sarah Orgel

THE DIFFICULT POEM

Often when students say they hate a poem they really mean that they don't understand it. They love Shel Silverstein because his work is instantly accessible. Our job as literature teachers is to make more challenging poems similarly comprehensible. This does not mean, however, that some poems won't continue to be difficult. As Charles Bernstein explained in a speech titled "The Difficult Poem,"

> I am the author of, and a frequent reader of, difficult poems. Because of this, I have the strong desire to help other readers and authors with hard-to-read poems. By sharing my experience of more than thirty years of working with difficult poems, I think I can save you both time and heartache. I may even be able to convince you that some of the most difficult poems you encounter can provide very enriching aesthetic experiences—if you understand how to approach them. (2003, 24)

Bernstein's approach involves the following assumptions:

- It is not your fault that difficult poems are difficult. In fact it is perceptive of a reader to discern that a poem may be hard to understand. Not being able to make sense of a poem on at first glance does not mean there is anything wrong with you.

◆ It is not the poem's fault that it is difficult. Many are quick to jump to judgment and declare a poem incoherent or meaningless simply because it is hard to understand. When a poem is difficult, there is not necessarily anything wrong with the poem.

Bernstein advises readers to stop blaming themselves or the poems and focus on the relationship between reader and text. As with any worthwhile relationship, this requires the investment of time and effort.

Teenagers being teenagers, they are loath to reread difficult poetry. The common *modus operandi* is to skim a poem lightly, then sit back and wait for the teacher to explain what it means. Knowing this, I try to create lessons that take students through the steps that a reader skilled in reading difficult poetry would instinctively take. If carefully crafted, such lessons can help students begin to develop a relationship with poetry. One poem that my tenth graders always find opaque on first reading is Robert Browning's "Meeting at Night."

MEETING AT NIGHT

The gray sea and the long black land;
And the yellow half-moon large and low;
And the startled little waves that leap
In fiery ringlets from their sleep,
As I gain the cove with pushing prow,
And quench its speed i' the slushy sand.

Then a mile of warm sea-scented beach;
Three fields to cross till a farm appears;
A tap at the pane, the quick sharp scratch
And blue spurt of a lighted match,
And a voice less loud, through its joys and fears,
Than the two hearts beating each to each!

Robert Browning

Rather than beginning our lesson with questions about the poem, I ask students to identify the imagery. I remind them that imagery is the representation of sensory experience in words and then draw a blank Sensory Images chart on the board (Figure 5.1). They copy the chart and the reread the poem to fill in words and phrases that appeal to sight, sound, touch, smell, taste, and movement.

Once students have worked alone for about ten minutes, I reread the poem aloud and ask them to contribute to our class compilation of Browning's sensory images. Each time a student offers an image, I ask what effect it had. What did they think it meant that the land was long and black and the moon large and low? Why were the waves "startled"? How might we interpret the "pushing prow"? The same students who would have complained that this was a stupid poem at first glance become eager participants in this interpretative game. Little by little, image by image, comprehension of the poem emerges. Before we have finished, students have created an entire story around these two lovers. One class was convinced that it is an illicit meeting and that the lovers are both married to someone else. "Mrs. Jago, why else would they be whispering? Why can't he just knock on the door?" "That's why she's afraid," I reply and suggest—and this may be a completely fanciful interpretation of mine—that the rhyme scheme supports this view. The *abccba* pattern is an unusual one that suggests to me two separated lovers who are briefly conjoined and then must separate. Most students roll their eyes at my idea but at least I get them to notice the rhyme scheme.

At the end of class, I always insist on a final reading of the poem. I want to make sure that we end with wholeness. Somehow "Meeting at Night" doesn't seem quite so difficult any more.

FIGURE 5.1   Sensory Images

Sensory Images in Robert Browning's "Meeting at Night"		
Sight	gray sea	blue spurt
	black land	leaping waves
	yellow half-moon	fiery ringlets
Sound	sound of waves	a voice less loud
	quick sharp scratch	hearts beating
	tap at the pane	
Touch	slushy sand	speed of boat
	tapping	
	warm beach	
Smell	sea-scented beach	
	smell of lit match	
	fields	
Taste		
Movement	pushing prow	
	fields to cross	

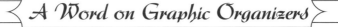

> I often use various charts and webs to help students make sense
> of what they read, but do not think it is a good idea to hand students
> blank graphic organizer forms. Creating an organizer in their own
> hand reinforces the idea that this is a tool to help them see relation-
> ships and make distinctions. Handing out blank forms inadvertently
> creates a dependence upon the teacher. I offer them a model but the
> "organizer" must be theirs.

INSPIRATION VERSUS PERSPIRATION IN EDGAR ALLAN POE'S "THE RAVEN"

I feel sure you didn't know that when Edgar Allan Poe sat down to write "The Raven," his first choice of bird was a parrot. This isn't one of those tall tales from literature but rather the author's own admission. A literary critic as well as a writer, Poe wondered why no writer had ever described in detail how a particular poem came to be, from inception to completion. He decided to do this for readers with his own best-known work, "The Raven." Scoffing at the romantic idea that poets work in a frenzy of ecstatic intuition, Poe explains that nothing in his poem is the result of "either accident or intuition. The work proceeded step-by-step, to its completion, with the precision and rigid consequence of a mathematical problem" (Matthews 1914).

To refresh your memory, the speaker in "The Raven" is lost in melancholic recollection of his lost love Lenore when suddenly startled by a knocking on the door. It is a raven who has come to visit "ever-more." Perching upon a bust of Pallas Athene, the raven responds to the saddened lover's increasingly tormented questions with a single word: "Nevermore."

Poe began his process of composition with form. He decided to write a poem of about one hundred lines. His next thought was for the impression or effect he wanted to convey. He chose Beauty. "Regarding, then, Beauty as my province, my next question referred to the tone of its highest manifestations—and all experience has shown that this tone is one of sadness. Beauty of whatever kind in its supreme development invariably excited the sensitive soul to tears. Melancholy is thus the most legitimate of all poetical tones." Following this decision, Poe turned to structure and decided that he needed a pivot upon which the poem would turn. He chose to employ a refrain, but a refrain that, while it would be repeated in terms of sound throughout the poem, would offer readers a variety of meanings. He wanted the refrain to be brief, even one word long, and felt that the sonorous long *o* sound would be the most suitable to carry his intentions. The result—"Nevermore."

Poe then had to devise a pretext for the refrain "Nevermore" to be repeated. "Here, then immediately arose the idea of a non-reasoning creature capable of speech, and very naturally, a parrot, in the first instance, suggested itself, but was superseded forthwith by a raven as equally capable of speech, and infinitely more in keeping with the intended tone." Having chosen this bird of ill omen for a character, Poe asked himself which topic was the most melancholy. The obvious answer was Death. From here it was a straightforward matter to link Beauty to Death through the death of a beautiful woman beloved by the poem's narrator.

Poe felt that "a close circumscription of space is absolutely necessary to the effect of an insulated incident—it has the force of a frame a picture." So the poem takes place within the narrator's chamber. Poe made the night tempestuous both to account for the Raven's seeking entry and to contrast with the serenity within the chamber. Why the bust of Pallas? "I made the bird alight on the bust of Pallas, also for the effect of contrast between marble and the plumage—it being understood that the bust was absolutely suggested by the bird—the bust of Pallas being chosen, first, as most in keeping with the scholarship of the lover, and secondly, for the sonorousness of the word, Pallas, itself."

Setting out to debunk the notion that poets work from inspiration rather than perspiration, Poe convinced this reader that literature is the result of both. A less inspired writer might well have stuck with the parrot.

6

Lesson Design for Classical Literature

ASSIGNING THE TITLE "Lesson Design" to this chapter makes me nervous. I have always been one of those free spirits who seem to make the lesson up as they go along. Offering a model for how a literature lesson could be taught seems antithetical to how I myself have always worked. Of course, when I "make it up" now, I am doing so from a deep knowledge of the literature and many years of classroom experience. Too many new teachers are thrown into the ring with little more than a list of books and an attendance roster. I say this not to point a finger at others but to describe the current state of affairs in most public high schools. I have served as English department chairperson at my high school on and off over the past fifteen years and know firsthand how little I have been able to help newly hired teachers. There simply isn't time. Some say of education that we are the only profession that eats its young. It doesn't need to be this way.

In *The Teaching Gap,* James W. Stigler and James Hiebert explain how one reason reforms in education fail is that they end up having almost no impact on the quality of teaching. They contend that it is teaching, not teachers, that must be changed. Stigler and Hiebert draw this conclusion from their observation of eighth-grade teachers and students participating in the Third International Mathematics and Science Study (TIMSS). They found that

> To improve teaching we must invest far more than we do now in generating and sharing knowledge about teaching. Compared with other countries, the United States clearly lacks a system for developing professional knowledge and for giving teachers the opportunity to learn about teaching. American teachers, compared with those in Japan, for example, have no means of contributing to the gradual improvement of teaching methods of improving their own skills. American teachers are left alone, an action sometimes justified on grounds of freedom, independence, and professionalism. This is not good enough if we want excellent schools in the next century. (1999, 13)

Most teachers model their practices on what they have observed during their many long years as a student. However much some assign blame to schools of education for their graduates' failure to raise test scores, the truth is that most of what new teachers know about teaching has come from their own experience of schooling. If we believe that instruction can and should be improved, we are going to have to look more closely at both how teachers learn and how to improve individual lessons.

FINDING A PROFESSIONAL HOME

In 1977 I was a third-year teacher at Lincoln Junior High. Though I liked teaching very much, my long-term plans did not include the classroom. My best friend was applying to law schools. I thought I might do the same. That spring the principal approached me to ask if I was interested in applying to be a fellow in a new summer program at UCLA. It was called the Writing Project. My guess is that the directors of the project tapped my school district as a likely partner for future work and invited them to suggest a teacher. My principal scanned the usual suspects and lighted on me. I accepted the invitation. I don't remember the application or interview but will never forget the first day of the institute. I was clearly the affirmative action fellow.

As you might expect, we began with introductions. All around the table were accomplished, professional teachers hungry to talk about writing. These were remarkable people with fifteen to twenty-five years of classroom experience and excellence all gathered in one room. I was a kid. Though I seemed to have an instinct for working with students and a lifelong passion for reading, what I knew about pedagogy could fit in a nutshell. Once introductions were over, I slipped out for a swim at the UCLA pool (membership at the recreation center was included in the fellowship) to decide whether or not to return.

Fortunately, the water assuaged my anxiety, and I went back. In many ways I have never left. Those 1977 UCLA Writing Project fellows were my teachers. They showed me what it meant to be a teacher in ways that my credential program and colleagues at Lincoln Junior High had never managed to. They inspired me. Rae Jean Williams, Ed Valentine, Jenee Gossard, Diane Dawson, Dick Dodge, Ruth Mitchell, and others set a standard of professional engagement that has stayed with me to this day. They helped me see that:

- Being a teacher means being a learner.
- However much you think you know, it is always worth thinking some more.
- Whenever you find yourself in a quandary, read the research.
- Teaching well can be thrilling.

James Gray, founder of the Bay Area Writing Project and later the National Writing Project, began with a simple and profound idea—successful teachers are the best teachers of teachers. This seems so obvious that it is hard to imagine that no one thought of it before. Yet this single idea has changed the nature of writing instruction. Over the past thirty years, thousands of teachers like me have attended Writing Project institutes and been transformed. This is not to suggest that institutes involve brainwashing or cult-like membership. The experience provides opportunities for reflecting on teaching practices. These occasions for learning happen over time, often over years. I know I didn't suddenly metamorphose into one of my fellow master teachers. I did learn how to become one through study, reflection, and a little help from my friends.

Ten years and a baby later, I took part in a teacher-researcher project under the tutelage of UCLA Writing Project director Faye Peitzman. I became enamored of the process, finding that writing about what I saw in my classroom helped me to be a more effective teacher. Always an over-achiever, I completed two studies that year. One focused on methods that seemed to help Latina students speak up in class. Though a handful of teachers at Santa Monica High School were angry that I should presume to suggest what was best for these young women, I am delighted to report that one of the students from that study is now my colleague, teaching Spanish and directing the school's AVID (Advancement Via Individual Determination) program.

The second teacher-researcher study whetted my appetite for publication. My article had one of the best titles I am ever likely to invent, "Flotation Strategies for Sinking Students" and was published in *English Journal.* There is nothing like being published to make you want to do it again. Of course writing was hard work but it never felt like extra work. Teacher research was helping me take classroom problems and turn them into worthy subjects for inquiry. It felt like spinning straw into gold.

Along with the foundational belief in teachers teaching teachers, the Writing Project model begins with the assumption that in order to be a successful writing teacher, one must write. When I arrived for that first Writing Project institute, I was a terrible writer. Everything about my writing was a mess: poor spelling, dangling modifiers, the entire range of mechanical errors. I was mortified. My writing group helped me see that with attention to detail my errors could be easily corrected. They helped me believe that what I possessed was special and deserved careful revision and editing—that I had something important to say.

Over the next twelve years I wrote a column for a local newspaper and then the Westside section of the *Los Angeles Times*. Writing about my students became an integral part of my teaching. When you have to produce 750 words each week, every week, you can't wait for a good idea. You have to take whatever idea presents itself. And it seemed that the more I wrote about what I saw in my classroom—the good, the bad, and the ugly—the better I understood how to teach. Donald Graves calls this a state of constant composition. The seed sown in a Writing Project summer institute so long ago was bearing fruit.

James Gray laid a foundation for what has become a national network, with 175 sites across the country, providing a professional home for thousands of teachers. Celebrating its thirtieth anniversary, the National Writing Project continues to thrive and grow. It now serves over 100,000 teachers in grades K–16 every year. Congress and President Bush approved a 2003 package that includes just under $17 million for NWP, an increase of $3 million over last year.

Big numbers like these are impressive and necessary for the network to continue its work, but the magic begins with ones and twos. One Writing Project fellow turns to a bright young teacher at her school and with a sparkle in her eye says, "Lasonya, you need to apply to the Writing Project this summer. I know you will love it. It's a chance to think about teaching with people who like to think." Those simple words repeated thousands of times over in fifty states, the District of

Columbia, Puerto Rico, and the U.S. Virgin Islands have improved the teaching of writing for untold numbers of children. I believe they have also kept many gifted teachers in the profession. Without a home like the National Writing Project, many of us would have been lost.

LESSON STUDY IN JAPAN

Professional development in Japan works very differently. Almost every elementary and middle school teacher in the country participates in *kounaikenshuu,* a series of activities that make up a comprehensive process of school improvement. Run by teachers, grade-level and subject matter groups meet regularly as part of their school day. A key component of this process is lesson study (*jugyou knkyuu*). Small groups of three to five teachers work together to design, implement, test, and improve what they call a "research lesson." The premise behind this process is simple.

> If you want to improve teaching, the most effective place to do so is in the context of a classroom lesson. If you start with lessons, the problem of how to apply research findings in the classroom disappears. The improvements are devised within the classroom in the first place. The challenge now becomes that of identifying the kinds of changes that will improve student learning in the classroom and, once the changes are identified, of sharing this knowledge with other teachers who face similar problems, or share similar goals, in the classroom. (Stigler and Hiebert 1999, 111)

This model attracts me because it is grounded in the classroom and recognizes that given the time and structure to do so, teachers can improve their practice. The TIMSS videotape project focused on mathematics classrooms, but with very little stretching the lesson studies can apply to literature lessons. The structure of the lesson study process varies, but the following steps are common:

Step 1: Defining the Problem

Teachers usually choose a problem they have identified in their own classroom. It can be as general as stimulating student interest in mathematics or as specific as improving students' understanding of how to add fractions with unlike denominators.

Step 2: Planning the Lesson

Teachers work together to design a lesson. Their goal is not only to plan an effective lesson but also to understand why and how the lesson promotes understanding for students.

Step 3: Teaching the Lesson

One teacher in the group demonstrates the lesson for her team. (You will be interested to learn that Japanese teachers can leave their classrooms without adult supervision for these observations. Student monitors keep order.)

Step 4: Evaluating the Lesson and Reflecting on Its Effect

The group meets after school on the day of the observation to debrief what they have seen. The teacher who gave the demonstration speaks first followed by critical comments from other members of the team. At all times the focus is on the lesson, not the teacher. As the lesson was designed collaboratively, all members of the team feel equally responsible for its strengths and weaknesses.

Step 5: Revising the Lesson

Teachers make changes to the original lesson taking into account the constructive criticism they received from peers.

Step 6: Teaching the Revised Lesson

This is often done by a different member of the team to a different group of students. All members of the school faculty are invited to watch the research lesson. The room can become very crowded.

Step 7: Evaluating and Reflecting Once More

The school faculty meets to discuss the lesson's goals and outcome. The focus is both on what students have learned and on what about teaching and learning can be drawn from the lesson.

Step 8: Sharing the Results

Unlike the United States, Japan has guidelines for a national curriculum. Successful research lessons are published and widely disseminated throughout the country. Some schools host a "lesson fair" where teachers from schools throughout a region come together to observe research lessons.

One of the most powerful outcomes of this lesson study process is that teachers develop a shared language for describing and analyzing classroom practices. It also involves all teachers at a school, not just the hardy few who attend professional conferences or read education journals. I think it holds real promise for improved teaching. In an interview for *Educational Leadership*, James Stigler explained:

> People in teaching take the mistaken view that "if I just do the standard practice, then I'm not being a professional. I need to do

something new, unique, creative." Al Shanker used to make this point quite powerfully. He said that what defines a profession is the standard practice. There's nothing wrong with going out and doing the standard practice, provided that you have a means of improving it over time. In medicine, if you don't follow the standard practice, they have a word for that: malpractice. Whereas in teaching, somehow we've promulgated the idea that a teacher is not a professional unless she invents it all by herself. (Willis 2002, 11)

If we implemented lesson study in this country it would mean that teachers don't have to make it all up alone. I recall the hours I have spent standing in line at our school Xerox machine. I think of my constant search for nonfiction passages to complement a particular novel or poem. Then I think of how many teachers have made this journey before me and probably have wonderful examples in their files. We simply never have the time to put our heads together. Americans ascribe virtue to individual effort and originality, but the longer I am in this profession, the more I am convinced that we need to spend more time working together toward a common goal.

It is in the spirit of lesson study that I offer the following lesson plans for teaching *The Odyssey*. Is it "teacher-proof"? Of course not. Anyone who thinks that instruction can be described step-by-step has never spent much time in the classroom. Even after twenty-nine years in the classroom I still can't write lesson plans for more than a week in advance. Teaching is an organic process, deeply dependent upon relationships between students and their teacher, students and the content, students and one another. Not to be responsive to the ever-changing demands of the young minds in my care is to abrogate my responsibility as a professional. It is also a recipe for classroom disaster. I completely agree with Linda Darling-Hammond that "the single most important determinant of success for a student is the knowledge and skills of that child's teacher" (Goldberg 2001, 689). Part of that skill is knowing when to proceed with the lesson at hand despite teenage whining for a day off since there is a pep assembly at noon and when to spot a teachable moment and spin it into gold.

Much of what appears here was developed in collaboration with my mentor Bill Clawson. I can no longer tell what is mine and what is his. Though some pieces of this unit have remained constant, my teaching of *The Odyssey* has never stopped changing. What I offer here is simply my latest—and I hope best—version. Use it as a jumping off place for designing your own lessons. As with Japanese research lessons, what follows will, I hope, provide ideas not only teaching *The Odyssey*, but for teaching any classic, challenging work of literature. As you read, consider how this plan for teaching Homer might be applied to Dickens, Orwell, Shakespeare, Dostoyevsky, Wharton, Huxley, García Márquez, Morrison, Hawthorne, or Austen. It is my hope that you can draw from my lesson insights that have implications for your teaching and your students' learning.

LESSON DESIGN FOR HOMER'S *ODYSSEY*

First, I need to address the translation of *The Odyssey* that I use. When I first began teaching the epic, I chose Albert Cook's 1967 translation published by W. W. Norton and Company. It is a particularly literal translation, though less beautiful in English than the more commonly used Robert Fitzgerald translation. If I were to choose again I would probably select the Fitzgerald version. What keeps me teaching from the Cook? These are the copies we have available in the textbook office. When new teachers join the department, I let them have the more recently purchased copies of the Fitzgerald translation. I mention this because I think it is sometimes difficult for those outside the hardscrabble world of public education to realize all the compromises teachers must make. My school can't afford to discard one hundred copies of perfectly good textbooks. Don't feel too sorry for me, though. I get to use the Seamus Heaney translation of *Beowulf* while the new teachers work from the Burton Raffel version.

The second thing I want to make clear is that while we teach *The Odyssey* in tenth grade, this does not mean that it can't be taught in the eighth, ninth, or twelfth grade. When Bill Clawson first began teaching the epic at Santa Monica High School, he chose to do it in the tenth grade because that was the class he taught. No ninth-grade teachers then or now wanted to include it in their curriculum. Most literature anthologies include excerpts from *The Odyssey* in their grade 9 books. What is important is that students should read this extraordinary and extraordinarily influential text. When that should best happen, I leave to your professional judgment and to that of those with whom you must compromise.

Entering an Epic

In order to teach a complex text like *The Odyssey,* you must first be familiar and conversant with the epic form. I always find that the more I know, the better able I am to make the reading comprehensible for students. The following is taken directly from M. H. Abrams' *A Glossary of Literary Terms*:

> **Epic.** In its strict sense the term *epic* or *heroic poem* is applied to a work that meets at least the following criteria: it is a long verse narrative on a serious subject, told in a formal and elevated style, and centered on a heroic or quasi-divine figure on whose actions depends the fate of a tribe, a nation, or the human race.
> Traditional epics were written versions of what had originally been oral poems about a tribal or national hero during a warlike

age. Among these are the *Iliad* and *Odyssey* that the Greeks ascribed to Homer; the Anglo-Saxon *Beowulf*, the French *Chanson de Roland* and the Spanish *Poema del Cid* in the twelfth century; and the thirteenth-century German epic *Nibelungenlied*. Literary epics are highly conventional compositions which usually share the following features, derived by way of the *Aeneid* from the traditional epics of Homer:

- The hero is a figure of great national or even cosmic importance.
- The setting of the poem is ample in scale. Odysseus wanders over the Mediterranean basin (the whole of the world known at the time), and in Book XI he descends into the underworld.
- The action involves superhuman deeds in battle or a long, arduous, and dangerous journey intrepidly accomplished, such as the wanderings of Odysseus on his way back to his homeland, in the face of opposition by some of the gods.
- In these great actions the gods and other supernatural beings take an interest or an active part.
- An epic poem is a ceremonial performance, and is narrated in a ceremonial style which is deliberately distanced from ordinary speech and proportioned to the grandeur and formality of the heroic subject and architecture. (1999, 76–77)

After handing out copies of *The Odyssey*, while there is still a sense of excitement in the air about a new book, I distill the information above into a short lecture. Students take notes using the Cornell Notes form (see Figure 6.1), which is used by teachers in all the discipline areas at my school. The consistency seems to help students know where to begin when asked to "take notes."

A Note on Note Taking

The most important reason for demanding that students take notes is to help them focus their attention on the material being presented. It may seem that it would be more efficient simply to copy and hand out the definition from Abrams and have them save this to study from. The problem with this plan for fifteen-year-olds is that once you hand them a paper, they don't think they need to read it. Even those who dutifully file it in a notebook hardly give it a glance. When students are taking notes, even copying what I've written on the board, they are attending to the information. With some classes you may need to collect these "notes" and even assign them a grade or points. I sometimes use a stamp. Always the notes are returned to students so that they can refer to them later. We pull out these epic notes again when beginning *Beowulf.*

Along with information about the epic as a genre, I also explain to students how *The Iliad* and *The Odyssey* were recited as entertainment and tell them about the role of the rhapsode, who would sing this story to his audience. I draw a feeble picture of a lyre on the board and have them copy this into their notes.

In order to situate their reading of *The Odyssey,* most students also need a quick retelling of the story of the Trojan War beginning with the judgment of Paris and his abduction of Helen. I don't ask students to take notes while I do this, but rather let them sit back and enjoy the story.

Beginning the Reading

Like all epics *The Odyssey* opens with an invocation to the Muse. In Greek mythology the Muses were the nine daughters of Zeus and

FIGURE 6.1   Cornell Notes

Cornell Notes	
Name _____	Period _____
Date _____ Subject _____ Introduction to *The Odyssey,* epics	
Questions/Comments Notes	

Mnemosyne. Originally there were only three, who were considered goddesses of memory—certainly good people to pray to as one embarked on a recitation of this length—though nine were later identified with individual arts. The Muses were not worshiped as deities but, rather, invoked by poets who called upon them for inspiration. Calliope is the particular Muse of epic poetry. "Tell me, Muse, about the man of many turns, who many / Ways wandered when he had sacked Troy's holy citadel" (1967a, 3).

An additional feature of epic poetry that students need to understand is the way the narrative starts *in medias res,* going directly to the heart of the matter. Following the invocation to the Muse, *The Odyssey* opens with an argument on Mount Olympus over what to do about Odysseus, who has been stranded on Ogygia for seven years. Only later, in Books IX through XII, will readers learn of the events that preceded his arrival on the nymph Calypso's island.

Many literature anthologies omit much of the first five books of *The Odyssey* on the assumption that students will have little patience for the squabbles of the gods or the background information regarding conditions at Odysseus' palace in Ithaca. Odysseus doesn't appear in the flesh until Book V. Anthologies have the constraints of page space to consider, but to experience the full impact of Homer's tale a reader needs to work through Books I–IV. To help ground our examination of methods for helping students do this work, here is a short summary.

The Story

The story begins on the island of Ogygia where Odysseus has been imprisoned by the nymph Calypso for seven years. She has offered him immortality in order to persuade him to remain with her, but Odysseus longs for Ithaca and his wife, Penelope.

The story then turns to Ithaca where suitors have been camping out in Odysseus' palace pursuing Penelope and indulging in wild parties at Odysseus' expense. Telemachos, Odysseus' son, is persuaded by Athene to take charge and plan a journey to look for his father. Not only is Telemachos a threat to the dangerous suitors, but he is also in need of experience of the outside world. In the guise of Menor Athene guides him to visit Nestor in Pylos and then Menelaus and Helen in Sparta. Both heroes fought in the Trojan War beside Odysseus. Menelaus tells Telemachos that he has heard that Odysseus is being held captive on Ogygia. He makes no mention of the nymph.

Meanwhile, under orders from Zeus, Calypso gives Odysseus the tools to construct a raft and set sail home. A storm brewed by Odysseus' archenemy, Poseidon, shipwrecks him in the land of the Phaeacians where he is befriended by the white-armed Nausicaa and her parents, Alcinous and Arete. At a banquet in the anonymous guest's honor, Odysseus reveals his identity and tells the tale of his journey from Troy to Calypso's island.

After sacking the city, Odysseus made a raid on the Ciconians where he lost a few of his companions. He then stopped in the Land of the Lotus-eaters where some of his men ate the lotus and thereby forgot their homes. Odysseus dragged them back to the ships and then stopped in the land of the Cyclops. Hoping to receive guest gifts, Odysseus falls into Polyphemus' trap and, along with his men, seems about to be eaten by the one-eyed monster, son of Poseidon. Odysseus blinds Polyphemus and escapes, but in the process incurs the wrath of the god of the sea. Reaching the island of Aeolus, Odysseus is given a bag of winds that his men make the mistake of opening, thinking that it contained treasure that Odysseus was hiding from them. The ship is blown back to Aeolus' island, but the king offers no further assistance. Back on the sea, the Laestrygonians then destroy all but one of Odysseus' ships. This sole vessel lands on Circe's island where the enchantress enjoys turning men into swine. Hermes gives Odysseus a magic herb called moly that makes him immune to her magic. Odysseus forces Circe to restore his men and remains with her for a year.

The death of one of his men by drunken misadventure persuades Odysseus that it is time to get back on the road. Circe tells him that he must descend into Hades and speak with Teiresias in order to learn what he must do to reach home. Odysseus then gets past Scylla and Charybdis with a loss of only six men and sails past the Sirens with no loss of life by putting wax in his men's ears and having them tie him to the mast so he can listen to the Sirens' song. The crew is then becalmed on Helios where they anger the gods by eating the sacred cattle. For this the ship is struck by a thunderbolt and only Odysseus survives, shipwrecked on Calypso's island.

After hearing his tale, the Phaecians shower Odysseus with gifts and escort him home to Ithaca on one of their magical ships. Disguised as a beggar, Odysseus tests the loyalty of his servants while he plots his revenge on Penelope's suitors. He is reunited with Telemachos and together they make a plan. With the help of Athene, the loyal swineheard Eumaeus, and Telemachos, Odysseus kills every suitor in the great hall of his palace. Odysseus makes the unfaithful serving girls clean up the mess and then hangs them for their disloyalty.

Odysseus and Penelope are reunited and Odysseus reestablishes himself as king of Ithaca.

For easy reference, *The Odyssey* can be divided into four major sections:

- Books I–IV, Telemachos' search for his father and himself
- Books V–VIII, Odysseus on Calypso's island and in the land of the Phaeacians

- Books IX–XII, Odysseus' adventures as told to the Phaeacians
- Books XIII–XXIV, Odysseus' homecoming and triumph

Comprehension Tools

Tools that help my students negotiate this unfamiliar world include a chart of the Greek gods, a map of Odysseus' journey, and a character web.

 Chart of the Greek gods.   I would hope that most students have some familiarity with the Greek gods, but this is not always the case. I create and have students copy into their notes a chart of the Greek gods for a quick review of names that will be appearing with regularity throughout our reading of *The Odyssey* (see Figure 6.2). The chart remains prominently displayed in the classroom for easy reference. Though you might want to refer as well to the gods' Roman names, I find that putting them on the chart complicates things for struggling readers. A list such as the following serves as an easy reference for students:

Aphrodite: goddess of love, beauty, and fertility
Apollo: god of poetry, music, prophesy, and healing
Ares: god of war and warlike frenzy
Artemis: virgin goddess of the hunt
Athene: goddess of wisdom, war, and peace.
Cronus: A Titan who ruled the universe until Zeus took over
Hephaestus: god of metalworking
Hades: god of the underworld, brother to Zeus
Hera: goddess of marriage, wife and sister of Zeus
Hermes: messenger god
Poseidon: god of the sea, brother of Zeus
Zeus: ruler, supreme god of all the Olympians

FIGURE 6.2   The Greek Gods

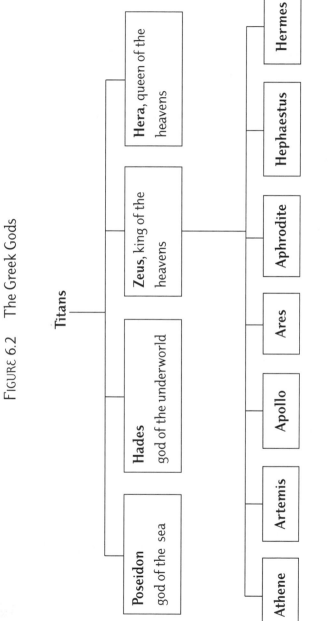

Map of Odysseus's Journey.   Any charting of Odysseus' wanderings is open to interpretation, yet a map seems to help my students envision where Odysseus has been and where he is going (see Figure 6.3). Few have any idea where Troy is in relation to Ithaca. In *Ulysses Found,* Ernle Bradford (1963) traces Odysseus' voyage in the modern Mediterranean. Bradford drew on his own seafaring skills and deep knowledge of the epic to deduce the locations where he believes Odysseus alighted. In the days when teachers still operated film projectors, I used to rent a gorgeous movie called *The Search for Ulysses* from our public library. In it, Bradford the sailor follows the path he believes Odysseus traveled. The film featured James Mason reading from *The Odyssey.* Alas! The film does not seem to have been transferred to video. The book *Ulysses Found* is out of print though still available in libraries and from used bookstores.

Character Webs.   One of the most challenging aspects of a complex piece of literature is retaining an accurate list of dramatis personae. In a text like *The Odyssey, Beowulf,* or *Crime and Punishment,* where character names sit uncomfortably on students' tongues, this is particularly troublesome. I construct the character web on chart paper and ask students to copy this web onto a large sticky note that they can place on the inside cover of their books for easy reference. As with the information on the epic, it might seem easier simply to duplicate the web in Figure 6.4 and hand it out to students, but I firmly believe that copying down these character names is a first step in making them familiar to students. We practice pronouncing the names together. How can students refer to characters in class discussions if they can't pronounce them? The large chart remains prominently displayed in front of the class for constant reference.

California English Language Arts Standard 3.3 says that students will "analyze interactions between main and subordinate characters and explain the way those interactions affect the plot" (1997). Though I once

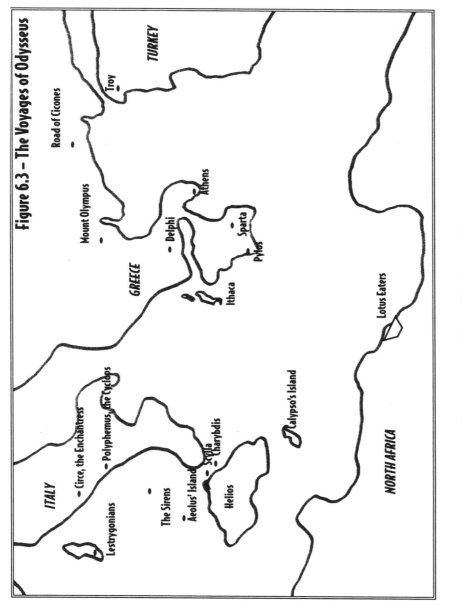

Figure 6.3 – The Voyages of Odysseus

FIGURE 6.3   Map of Odysseus' Journey

FIGURE 6.4   *The Odyssey*: A Cast of Characters

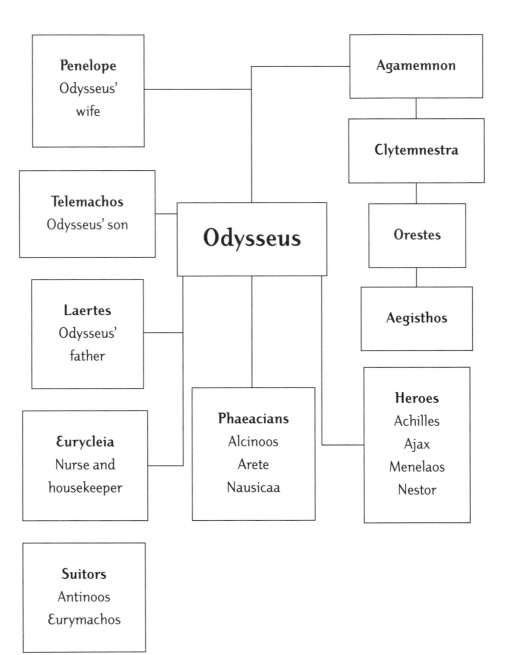

scoffed at the idea of posting state standards around the classroom, I've come to see the value of displaying a standard beside our character webs and other displays of our work in progress. Such signs seem to make clear to both students and visitors that our work is truly standards-aligned.

Epic Style

Epic style features two particular elements: epithets and epic similes.

Epithets

> **Epithets:** short, stock adjective or adjectival phrase that defines a distinctive quality of a person or thing.

In Homer, epithets are often reoccurring, as in the *wine-dark sea, many-minded Odysseus, cloud gathering Zeus,* and of course *early-born, rosy-fingered dawn.* In order to draw students' attention to style, I ask them to collect epithets as they read Book II. At the beginning of class we go around the room and each student reads out one epithet from the text trying not to repeat what has been said before. Our class list often looks something like this:

early-born, rosy-fingered dawn
long-haired Achaians
swift-footed dogs
godlike Odysseus
godly Odysseus
ill-fated man
Zeus-born Odysseus
winged words
Ithacan Odysseus
life-killing drug

Olympian Zeus
well-greaved Achaians
high-talking Telemachos
sound-minded Telemachos
sea-circled Ithaca
long-sorrowful death
fair-braided Achaians
many-voiced assembly
scepter-bearing king
high-roofed chamber
well-timbered ship
wine-faced sea
well-plaited oxhide ropes
bright-eyed Athene

I want to draw students' attention to this feature of Homer's style early so that they will begin to notice how often these epithets are repeated. This repetition was an aide to the rhapsodes in performance and provided listeners with quick characterizations of characters and snapshots of settings. Extending the lesson, I ask students to make up epithets for a family member, a pet, a coach, a political figure, and a movie star. Playing with epithets in this manner seems to strengthen students' understanding of their artistic purpose. A strict band director was labeled "time-beating Sakow." A popular cross-country coach "flat-footed Coach Cady," A nagging mother "shrill-voiced Leona." Tenth graders are quick to spot shortcomings in the adults who wield power over them. I always make students promise that what they hear will stay within the room.

As they play with Homer's language, students find that it feels less foreign. I invite them to imitate the first sixteen lines of *The Odyssey* imagining that this was the opening to an epic about their lives. How might a rhapsode begin? Ethan Hutt wrote:

Tell me, Muse about the man of many miles,
Who many times dashed as he ran through the streets of Santa
Monica. He saw the Fatigue of his teammates and knew their pain.
On the course, he too suffered great pains within his lungs,
Yearning for the finish line, and his teammates' success.
He could not guide his team to victory, though he wanted to:
His teammates had lost the race because of their laziness.
The slackers had disregarded the wise words
Of the well-traveled coach Cady, who knew the path to victory.
Tell the tale for us, beginning with the previous day,
Sometime after the piercing bell had sounded.
When all the others, seeking refuge from the torments of school
Had fled, light-footed to the safety of their homes.
Yet he alone, longing for the final mile and his own return,
Was confined by sound-minded Coach Cady, who strives for
excellence,
To the fenced-in, crimson rubber surface that was his training
ground.

A brilliant, overachieving tenth grader, Etha Williams turned in the following to me last fall. When she read this to the class, the other students
and I were awestruck. "Samohi" refers to the nickname of our school,
Santa Monica High School. "AcaDeca" refers to the Academic
Decathalon.

Sing to me, O Muse, of the girl of hurried ways and multi-tasking,
Etha, to whom unknowing mortals said, "There's no way you'll do
all that."
Their voices sincere and mild, yet full of demon lies.
For as children who have been taught malicious lies speak vile ser-
pent words

In sweet voices full of pure innocence, hope, and love,
So did those at Samohi, people of every kind, scoff at Etha's ways.
Let the Muses through me give witness to the exploits through
which she went,
And her success, as omnipresent as the gods themselves, in man-
aging to do it all.
With Etha no time was wasted, no energy spared, not a fragment of
a moment left unforgotten;
One fair fall morning, rosy-fingered Dawn had scarcely graced the
sheets of endless sky
With her endless streams of golden paint and dewdrop kisses
Before Etha's agitated feet, with energy equaled only by winged
Hermes,
Carried her into the crowded classroom of many-minded Mr.
Gaida,
Teacher of AP Bio and AcaDeca. It is of these courses that students
cry out,
"As mortal men would struggle with the great tasks of Hercules,
So we struggle as we learn the incalculable masses of material for
our upcoming tests."
Yet Etha, girl of hurried ways, let no amount of difficulty stop her
in her ways;
Even as the bell rang out cruelly, even as many-minded Mr. Gaida
gave great work,
She whipped her calculator out of her backpack with a frenetic
kind of speed
And began to work concurrently: for even as she analyzed great
knows in biology
She also wove her way through lacy mazes of matrices. This she
did with great care;
For as when but one problem is mistakenly skipped on the SAT

Every answer thenceforth becomes incorrect and an entire future
is forsaken

So does a simple mistake in calculation, tiny yet enormous, ruin
completely

The answer to a woven mass of numbers, a matrix, so inexpressively intricate.

In this way did Etha work, doing both, and doing both well, yet with
speed.

Her eyes at last darted up. They, too, possessed the strange hurriedness.

All she saw was the stark white clock, hands ticking cruelly: one
minute left.

And as a man, sensing that his journey over the River Styx is imminent, makes haste

In order that he finish everything he has set out to do in this world,

So did multi-tasking Etha in this last minute hurry mightily to finish the last of the lacy matrixes.

Her hand was bringing the end of the last matrix towards the end
as the tone sounded.

Victory, thought the girl of hurried ways; I have won, Etha the
multi-tasker gloated.

The song of Nike filled her heart, and she was not a little bit smug.

Then held the great gods counsel on Mount Olympus. It was a time
of great war

And the gods interfered rarely with mere mortals' lives.

Yea as bright-eyed Athene gazed down upon the girl of multi-tasking

She perceived her self-satisfaction, and she felt a cold anger seeping into her own heart.

Then did she bring her anger before the assembly of the gods:

"Etha must not be allowed to sit there any longer, gloating and
feeling smug

At her own ability and wit. Has she not heard vain Arachne's tale?
Has she learned nothing?
As I brought terrible consequence upon that wretched once-woman
Who dared to feel pleased not with the gods, but with herself,
Who loved her weaving, that of men, rather than my weaving, that
which is divine,
So will I smite Etha for this insolence she shows unto me,
That she might see how pallid her talents are beside mine own."
Hera, wife of Zeus, pleaded in turn:
"My child, what sort of word has gotten past the bar of your teeth?
Show mercy, and show moderation; for the girl has not directly
offended you.
She has only been a little pleased with herself, and has not boasted
of exceeding you
In wit, or wisdom, or in anything. Perhaps she is mistaken in her
thoughts,
But the rage you give her should not be so harsh. Do not punish
her; but if you must,
Allow her more mercy, at least, than you showed vain Arachne in
her day."
Bright-eyed Athene made no response; but in her actions, she
relented.
She turned Etha into no base animal; she made the girl of hurried
ways suffer no great pains;
She merely came down in spirit form, invisible and unfathomable,
and,
While always hurrying Etha quickly jammed her notebook into her
backpack,
In an almost imperceptible motion bright-eyed Athene knocked
Etha's mocha over.
And, as a wave from the ocean strikes without discrimination,
Hitting the cold sand and the poor man's last loaf of bread alike,

So did the mocha's contents spill everywhere—on Etha's desk and chair

But also on her teacher's eighty-dollar graphing calculator.

But Etha was busy, struggling against her notebook to force it down quickly

And she noticed nothing of bright-eyed Athene's actions.

Even so, bright-eyed Athene was smiling from Mount Olympus,

For Etha's noticing the situation was imminent, and her seeing this,

Ostensibly the product of her hurried actions and pell-mell multi-tasking,

Would dissolve some of her pride, some of that smugness Athene so despised.

As these events transpired, sound-minded Tanya, Etha's good friend, entered.

Etha bade her a mumbled greeting as she continued the struggle with her notebook.

She was in no mood to speak; the notebook wasn't cooperating, and it was growing late.

But even through her own frustration she heard the doom in Tanya's words:

"Oh no . . . Etha . . . " were the only words which Etha heard before she gazed up and saw the mocha running along the desk, on the graphing calculator, off the desk,

In a path resembling a muddy river overridden by pollution.

For a moment ugly Chaos seized her spirit; she knew not what to do.

She rubbed the calculator on her jacket; to no avail,

The Fates had dressed her in a jacket whose cloth was not absorbent.

"Will a four-dollar drink destroy an eighty-dollar machine?"

As summer persistently comes each year, so did worries come to Etha,

Hurrying every moment, hurrying even more as she imagined telling about it—

Explaining to her father, the son of Savonus, God of Cheap, what she had done.

Panic seized Etha by the soul, and she became more hurried than ever;

She muttered a hurried prayer: "O ye gods

Grant me but one thing: a solution to this problem, and I will be eternally grateful.

I will pour out libations to you in mochas and espressos and café au laits

Every morning when I drink my coffee and at all other times when coffee touches my lips."

Hopelessly, she peered around, at last slowing down slightly, expecting nothing.

And then something on the counter, buried under posters caught her eye—

As a man who is about to be found guilty for a murder he did not commit feels

When new DNA evidence reveals that he could not have been the killer

So did Etha feel as she gazed upon this thing, a small dirty rag

Whose existence saved her eight weeks of allowance and countless vituperative words.

She grabbed it violently and ran back to her desk,

Attacking with a strange vicious urge the splotches of mocha on the calculator,

She worked with speed; at last it was done; the calculator worked; the area was clean.

Always hurrying Etha threw the calculator into her backpack and began to run.

She felt her shoes treading dangerously quickly down the science building stairs;

She nearly slipped and noted inwardly that if she did, it would excuse the tardy;

Ran the shortest way to the English building, kicking dirt into her nose;

Ran up a flight of stairs, legs tired, and pushed open the Humanities Center door.

As a man feels when he enters the Elysian Fields,

So did hurrying Etha feel that day as she rushed to her seat and put down her backpack, weary after the rush.

Etha's breathing was quick; her movements were quicker; and her temper was quickest of all.

I can only bear witness to such work and be grateful to the gods who send me students like Etha.

Epic Similes

Epic similes compare heroic events in the story with common, everyday events. The challenge for my students is that many of the things that were everyday experiences for Homer's audience—for example, a man with a torch in a field—are as unfamiliar to them as Odysseus hiding in a pile of leaves. "As a man may cover a torch with black embers / At the edge of a field, where no neighbors may be by, / And save the fire's seed, so he need not light it from elsewhere. / So Odysseus covered himself with leaves" (78). Epic similes are sometimes quite long, offering the poet the opportunity to spin out a detailed comparison. The most famous of these in *The Odyssey* is Homer's comparison of the blinding of Polyphemus with the work of a carpenter and blacksmith.

They lifted the olive pole that was sharp at its tip

And thrust it in his eye; I myself, leaning on it from above,
Twirled it around as a man would drill the wood of a ship
With an auger, and others would keep spinning with a strap beneath,
Holding it at either end, and the auger keeps on going.
So we held the fire-sharpened pole in his eye
And twirled it. The blood flowed around it, hot as it was.
The fire singed his eyebrows and eyelids all around
From the burning eye. Its roots swelled in the fire to bursting,
As when a smith plunges a great ax or an adz
Into cold water and the tempering makes it hiss
Loudly, and just that gives the strength to the iron;
So did his eye sizzle around the olive pole. (124)

In order to imprint the epic simile "As . . . So . . . " pattern on students' minds, I hand students a collection of six epic similes from *The Odyssey* and have student groups take one and explain the comparison to the class. (See Figure 6.5 on page 128 for the assignment.) Often student groups choose to act out or to make a drawing of the epic simile. After groups have unpacked these examples of Homeric poetry, we talk about what all the similes had in common and what purpose they serve within the epic. They inevitably construct the very definition that I want them to know.

Epic Details

Homer paints a vivid picture of life during the Bronze Age (1100–1200 B.C.). A German archeologist, Heinrich Schliemann, excavated both Mycenae in Greece and Troy in western Turkey and found in Troy a city that resembles closely Homer's description of Troy in *The Iliad*. Throughout both epics are extended descriptions of how people sat down to banquets, prepared for war, loaded boats, did their laundry, and offered libations to the gods. These descriptions are sometimes referred

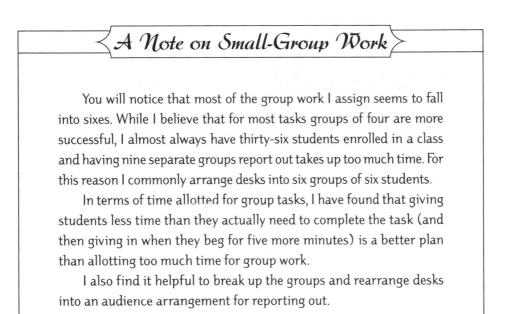

> ### ⟨ A Note on Small-Group Work ⟩
>
> You will notice that most of the group work I assign seems to fall into sixes. While I believe that for most tasks groups of four are more successful, I almost always have thirty-six students enrolled in a class and having nine separate groups report out takes up too much time. For this reason I commonly arrange desks into six groups of six students.
>
> In terms of time allotted for group tasks, I have found that giving students less time than they actually need to complete the task (and then giving in when they beg for five more minutes) is a better plan than allotting too much time for group work.
>
> I also find it helpful to break up the groups and rearrange desks into an audience arrangement for reporting out.

to as *epic details*. At the end of Book I, Eurycleia the house servant, "folded up the tunic, put it in smooth order / And hung it on a peg beside the jointed bed. / Then she went out of the bedroom, drew the door shut with a ring / Of silver, and drew the bolt full length by its thong" (15). By the time students complete their reading of *The Odyssey* they should have a vivid picture in their minds of the aspects of life in Mycenean times that Homer chose to describe.

Character Analysis: Odysseus

If I were asked to identify the moment when *The Odyssey* comes alive for most students, I would have to say it occurs when the character of Odysseus becomes real to them. Since he doesn't appear until Book V, this requires some tap dancing on the part of the instructor. I try to help them identify with Telemachos' plight: growing up in a single-parent

FIGURE 6.5   Understanding Epic Similes

Your task

Read the epic simile assigned to your group. Talk about the comparison Homer is making between a familiar experience and an event in *The Odyssey*. Prepare to present your explanation to the class. You have ten minutes to work.

Group 1

Then he hastened upon the wave as a sea gull does
That over the terrible gulfs of the barren sea
Dips its rapid wings, while catching fish, in the brine.
Like one of these, Hermes bore himself over many waves. (66)

Group 2

As when the North Wind at harvest time carries thistles
Over the plain, but they hold close to one another,
So the winds carried it here and there over the sea. (73)

Group 3

As when a blustering wind shakes up a heap
Of dry husks, and scatters them in all directions,
So it scattered the raft's long beams. (74)

Group 4

As when it appears delightful to sons if their father lives, who
Lies in sickness and undergoes strong pains,
Long wasting away, and some dread god has assailed him,
Whom now the gods have delightfully freed from misfortune;
So delightful did land and forest appear to Odysseus. (75)

Group 5

As when an octopus is pulled out of its den,
Numerous pebbles are caught in its suckers,
So against the rocks the skin from his stout hands
Was stripped off. (76)

(continues)

Group 6

As a woman weeps embracing her beloved husband

Who has fallen before his own city and his own people,

Warding off from city and children the pitiless day,

And she sees the man dying and breathing heavily,

And falls down upon him and piercingly shrieks. The enemy

From behind strike her back and her shoulders with spears

And lead her off in bonds to have trouble and woe,

And her cheeks are wasted for her most wretched grief;

Just so did Odysseus shed a piteous tear under his eyebrows. (111)

---

home, never knowing his father, surrounded by his mother's suitors, never having been outside his hometown.

Once we reach Book V, I focus on fleshing out the character of Odysseus. California English Language Arts Standard 3.4 (1997) says that students will determine characters' traits by what the characters say about themselves in narration and dialogue. I address this by drawing an open mind on the board and asking students to contribute the character traits they observed from their reading. (See Figure 6.6.) While I add their suggestions to the outline on the board, I ask students to create their own. This helps to ensure that everyone is paying attention. At every step and with every suggestion I ask students to offer lines from the text that support the trait they proffer. One of the exciting aspects of this exercise is that they quickly begin to see how Odysseus is a mass of contradictions. This is one of the reasons he is such a fascinating character. Feminists in the class are often angered by Odysseus' professed loyalty to Penelope while carrying on with other women (Calypso, Circe, the Sirens). This topic makes for rich classroom discussion. As our reading progresses, we add to our open mind until a full portrait of the complex hero emerges.

A Note on Visualizing Fictional Worlds

Whether the text is *Great Expectations, Julius Caesar,* or *Lord of the Flies*, students need to "see" the fictional worlds in which Dickens, Shakespeare, and Golding have set their stories. Sometimes students' lack of engagement is a result of not having situated characters in time and place. All action seems to occur in an incomprehensible vacuum. It is essential for teachers to help students re-create the fictional world. Drawing attention to descriptive passages in the opening pages is useful. So is pointing out key indicators of setting like clothing, modes of transportation, architecture, landscape, and weather. When I teach Victor Hugo's *The Hunchback of Notre Dame*, I always show the first six minutes of the Charles Laughton 1939 version so that students can see the cathedral and clothe the characters. I don't want to do all the work for them, but without a little help, some students will do no work at all. When they tell you a book is "stupid" what they sometimes mean is that they can't visualize this fictional world.

Homework

Almost invariably, when I start talking about homework, someone tells me that homework is a middle-class notion, and that as long as I make out-of-class reading a requirement for success, some students will be doomed to failure. I cannot accept this. While it may be true that many students face enormous obstacles to completing their homework, I refuse to solve the problem by minimizing homework assignments. It is not possible to teach classical literature to students who will not read outside of class. Some teachers try to solve this problem by carving out class time for reading, but even one day a week or fifteen minutes a day will decrease the time you have for discussion and interaction by 20 percent. Students need to do their homework reading.

FIGURE 6.6   Odysseus' Open Mind

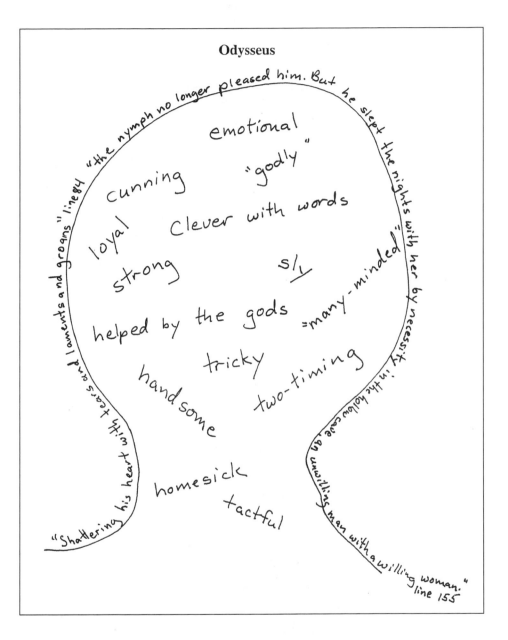

Odysseus

"the nymph no longer pleased him. But he slept the nights with her by necessity, in the hollow cave an unwilling man with a willing woman." line 155

lines 84 "the nymph no longer pleased him"

and laments and groans"

"Shattering his heart with tears

emotional

cunning   "godly"

loyal   clever with words

strong   sly

helped by the gods   =many-minded

tricky

handsome   two-timing

homesick

tactful

Given the competing demands on students outside class—math homework, sports, family responsibilities, television, and their ubiquitous cell phones—I find that I must occasionally play "Gotcha!" with students and give quizzes on their homework reading. Anyone who has stared out at a sea of blank faces hoping they won't be called on will understand why this is necessary. I don't weight these quizzes very heavily in terms of students' grades (please don't tell my students this), but they worry when they receive a paper with a fat zero, and I try to use that worry to make them put down the phone and pick up their books.

You can easily construct a quiz by taking a few key lines from the end of the homework assignment and asking students to write for three to five minutes on how this relates to what has gone before. I tell students who have not completed the reading not to make up a fairy story but instead to copy the following sentence onto their papers, "I promise with all my heart to make up the reading and come to class tomorrow prepared." On other occasions I hand out simple, plot-based quizzes like the one below.

Quiz on Book I of The Odyssey.   Answer the following questions on a separate sheet. You may not use your book.

1. Describe how you imagined Athene in your mind's eye as you read (character, attitude, looks, tone of voice).
2. Where is Odysseus at the moment? Why is he there?
3. What does Athene ask her father for help with?
4. What kind of a young man does Telemachos seem to be?
5. Explain the purpose of Athene's visit to Ithaca.
6. What textual challenges did reading *The Odyssey* pose for you last night?
7. What reading strategies might you employ to help you understand what you read tonight? (Please don't say "Check out SparkNotes"!)

The last parenthetical comment on SparkNotes and other such online study guides raises an important issue when teaching any classical work. Students have at their fingertips summaries of almost all the literature we teach in school. Instead of decrying this development, I make students aware of these resources. Doing so suggests to them that I've read them all (which I haven't) and puts them on notice that I am aware of what is out there. We talk about how relying on such predigested material is like letting someone else chew your food for you. There will be emergencies when a student may be forced to reach for this kind of help, but it should be just that—an emergency—rather than standard operating procedure.

Quiz on Book V of The Odyssey.   Answer the following questions on a separate sheet. You may not use your book.

- Explain the basic situations of Odysseus, Penelope, and Telemachos at the beginning of *The Odyssey.*
- Describe the suitors. What is their goal?
- What is the function of the assembly that opens Book II?
- What role does Athene play with Telemachos in Books I–III?
- Who is Nestor and how does he know Odysseus?
- What happened to Agamemnon when he returned home from the Trojan War?
- Why is Calypso angry with the gods?
- Why does Poseidon wish to destroy Odysseus?

You will notice that in the directions I specifically forbid students to use their books. The purpose of these quizzes is to reward those who have read and give pause to those who have not. I have to state this clearly because for almost every other kind of assessment I give students, using their books is not only allowed but encouraged.

An assignment that checks for understanding and sends students back to the pages they read for homework is a "What's Important" worksheet (see Figure 6.7). By asking students to select an important line or lines, I help them see that not all lines are of equal importance. As they work through restating their chosen quotation and then explaining its importance, first to the text and then to themselves, students' understanding of the lines deepens. Once they finish the task I have them share what they have written with a partner and then call on a few students to read their comments to the whole class. I collect their papers, though only to send the message that their work is important.

Comparing Translations

Many of the classical texts we teach were originally written in a foreign language. Once students have become comfortable with the translation we are reading, I shake them up a bit by showing them how differently other translators have rendered Homer's lines. Together we read and discuss the following translations of the conclusion to Book IX where Polyphemos the Cyclops prays to his father, Poseidon, to punish Odysseus for blinding him.

Albert Cook translation (1967)
Hear me, earth-girding Poseidon of the dark-blue locks,
If truly I am yours, and you declare you are my father,
Grant that the city-sacker Odysseus not go homeward,
The son of Laertes whose home is in Ithaca.
But if it is his fate to see his dear ones and arrive
At his well-established home and his fatherland,
May he come late and ill, having lost all his companions,
On someone else's ship, and find troubles at home.

FIGURE 6.7   What's Important?

Copy an important line or lines from last night's reading.	
Restate the lines in your own words.	
Why are these lines important to the passage?	
Why are they Important to you?	

Robert Fitzgerald translation (1952)

O hear me, lord, blue girdler of the islands
if I am thine indeed, and thou art father:
grant that Odysseus, raider of cities, never
see his home: Laertes' son, I mean,
who kept his all on Ithaka. Should destiny
intend that he shall see his roof again
among his family in his father land,
far be that day, and dark the years between.
Let him lose all companions, and return
under strange sail to bitter days at home.

E. V. Rieu translation (1946)

At this the Cyclops lifted up his hands to the heavens that hold the
stars and prayed to the Lord Poseidon: "Hear me, Poseidon, Girdler
of Earth, god of the sable locks. If I am yours indeed and you
accept me as your son, grant that Odysseus, who styles himself
Sacker of Cities and son of Laertes, may never reach his home in
Ithaca. But if he is destined to reach his native land, to come late,
in evil plight, with all his comrades dead, and when he is landed,
by a foreign ship, let him find trouble in his home.

Richmond Lattimore translation (1967)

So I spoke, but he then called to the lord Poseidon
in prayer, reaching both arms up toward the starry heaven:
"Hear me, Poseidon who circle the earth, dark-haired. If truly
I am your son, and you acknowledge yourself as my father,
grant that Odysseus, sacker of cities, son of Laertes,
who makes his home in Ithaka, may never reach that home;
but if it is decided that he shall see his own people,
and come home to his strong-founded house to his own country,

let him come late, in bad case, with the loss of all his companions, in someone else's ship, and find troubles in his household.

Samuel Butler translation (1900)

On this he lifted up his hands to the firmament of heaven and prayed, saying, "Hear me, great Neptune; if I am indeed your own true-begotten son, grant that Ulysses may never reach his home alive; or if he must get back to his friends at last, let him do so late and in sore plight after losing all his men let him reach his home in another man's ship and find trouble in his house."

Alexander Pope translation (1726)

Hear me, O Neptune; thou whose arms are hurl'd
From shore to shore, and gird the solid world.
If thine I am, nor thou my birth disown,
And if th' unhappy Cyclop be thy son,
Let not Ulysses breathe his native air,
Laertes's son, of Ithaca fair!
If to review his country be his fate,
Be it thro' toils and suff'rings, long and late;
His lost companions let him first deplore;
Some vessel, not his own, transport him o'er;
And when at home from foreign suff'rings freed,
More near and deep, domestic woes succeed!

My students invariably like the Pope translation best for its emphasis on meter and rhyme.

To the extent possible, I always try to offer students a sense of what the text is like in the original. I have the good fortune to be able to bring my husband, a classical scholar, to class to read passages from *The Odyssey* in Greek. For Edmund Rostand's *Cyrano de Bergerac,* I show a clip from the 1990 Gerard Depardieu version with the subtitles turned off. I almost always have in class a Russian student who can give us the flavor of *Crime and Punishment* in the original. Your school or public library probably owns a recording of *Beowulf* in Old English. You can also hear a selection of Old English read online by Steve Pollington at <*www.kami.demon.co.uk/gesithas/readings/readings.html*>. I don't want students to forget that what we are reading is in translation.

Students Take Over the Teaching

When I am teaching *The Odyssey* or any other classical work, I teach intensely the first third to half of the book but then turn the teaching over to students. I expect them to have internalized the methods we have used for unlocking the meaning in the text and be able to employ them on their own. I structure this by teaching *Odyssey* Books I–XII intensely and then assigning small groups of students individual books to present to the class (see Figure 6.8). Their assignment is to teach the class, not stage a performance. I believe that by learning one book of *The Odyssey* deeply and independently they will develop the confidence to read other challenging texts. I want them to see that with a little help from their friends, they can do it without me. I want to move their Zone of Proximal Development one stage further along. It requires students to work outside their Zone of Minimal Effort. No more sitting back and expecting Mrs. Jago to have all the answers and do all the work.

As you can see from the schedule, the pacing of the reading is quite brisk during this period. My feeling is that teachers often beat a text to death by investing as much scrutiny to the second half of the book that they do to the first. If students haven't developed the skills to begin to sail along under their own steam, I haven't done my job very well. Will some take a budget tour through these pages or resort to Cliffs Notes? Possibly, though it won't be enough for the book they are teaching to the class. More important than ensuring that every student

FIGURE 6.8   Presentation Chart

Odyssey **Presentations**

Your Goals

To summarize the important action and ideas in your assigned book

To present those ideas in a lively, engaging manner

To help your classmates understand the text

To expand our thinking about the epic as a whole

Requirements

You must hand in a written summary of the book when you present.

Presentation should be twenty to twenty-five minutes in duration and involve the class in some way.

Please be responsible for keeping up with the reading so that you can be an involved participant for others.

Book assigned	Date of presentation	Group members
XIII	October 2	Jake, Jessica, Kristen, Destiny
XIV	October 2	Sara, Sunil, Emily, Adrienne
XV	October 3	Erica, David, Alana
XVI	October 3	Natasha, Quaneise, Cooper
XVII	October 5	Sarve, Elliot, Rosa
XVIII	October 5	Lucy, Michael, Ruth, José
XIX	October 8	Jerzy, Amara, Jackson
XX	October 8	Greg, Mary, Elena, James
XXI	October 9	Tim, Amanda, Brian, Jarin
XXII	October 9	Daniel, Margaret, Daniel, Dionna
XXIII	October 11	Mrs. Jago
XXIV	October 12	Mrs. Jago
TEST	October 15	All

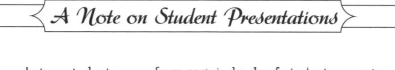

A Note on Student Presentations

I steer students away from certain kinds of student presentations, not because they aren't engaging but because experience with them has shown me that they don't result in deep learning or textual analysis. Examples include

1. A game show format with students handing out candy for correct answers on trivial questions from their book
2. Puppet shows (too much time spent cutting and gluing and not enough spent thinking)
3. Poster presentations full of images from the Internet, sometimes unread

The goal of the presentation must always be to deepen their classmates' understanding of *The Odyssey*. No points for cute.

read every word is ensuring that every student knows how to read an epic.

Not all works of literature divide up so tidily. For most other texts I often ask the class to complete the reading over a long weekend or vacation break and then assign students to "expert groups." Their assignment is once more to teach the class what they have learned through intense scrutiny of a key question. The questions must be large ones, the kind that one might write a whole essay on and the group's task is to engage the class in a rich conversation of the subject. The group must cull the text for important quotations to support the discussion. To give you a sense of the kinds of questions I mean, here are the ones I use for Edmund Rostand's *Cyrano de Bergerac:*

Expert Group Assignments

Expert Group 1

How does Rostand prepare the audience for Cyrano's death and the resolution of his relationship with Roxanne?

Expert Group 2

How is Cyrano's gesture of throwing away the bag of gold in Act I characteristic of him? Is it symbolic? Does he do similar things elsewhere in the play? Discuss Cyrano's character in light of this gesture.

Expert Group 3

Discuss how the following characters do or don't change over the course of the play: DeGuiche, Roxanne, Ragueneau, Christian, Cyrano.

Expert Group 4

Is Cyrano a tragic or pathetic character? Be sure to define what you mean by each of these terms.

Expert Group 5

How does the attitude of the cadets toward Cyrano shed light on Cyrano's character?

Expert Group 6

Much of this play is concerned with the conflict between appearance and truth. Discuss Rostand's use of irony.

For many tenth graders such questions, if assigned on a test or for an essay, would probably lie outside their Zone of Proximal Development and be much too difficult for them to tackle alone. With the help of their peers and in a structured environment with me circulating among the groups and pointing to places in the play where they might find the answers they seek, students are able to rise to the task.

Beyond the Text

Given that my instructional goal for teaching a text like *The Odyssey* is not only to get students *through* the text but also to teach them *how* to read challenging literature, I always ask students as we finish the epic what advice they would give to next year's students. Teenagers love giving advice. What I like about the exercise is that it deepens students' understanding of the processes they used to comprehend the text. It always amuses me to hear the things I nagged them about coming out of their mouths as advice. Here's the list last year's class compiled. You can imagine how delighted I was to see the bullet on breaking up their reading with thinking.

Advice on How to Read Homer's *Odyssey*

1. Read on a nightly basis. Don't fall behind. The class discussions will be more beneficial to you this way.
2. Keep your character chart handy.
3. Read out loud.
4. Picture what you are reading in your head.
5. Read slowly. Take your time to understand.
6. Break up your reading with thinking.
7. Read in an uncomfortable position. Drink coffee.
8. Reread parts you don't understand.
9. Participate in class discussions. Bring questions.
10. Think about what you read outside of class.
11. Relate what is going on in the story to your own life.

My hope is that students internalize the advice they have for others and apply it the next time they pick up a challenging text.

I also want students to see how their newly acquired knowledge of *The Odyssey* can be immediately applied to reading other works that allude to Homer's tale. The best-known of these, of course, is James Joyce's *Ulysses* but as these fifteen-year-olds are not quite ready for that text, we read Tennyson's "Ulysses." Before I hand out copies of the poem I ask them what they think Odysseus would be feeling a couple of years down the road. Their speculations seem to prepare them well for Tennyson's take on the matter.

ULYSSES

by Alfred, Lord Tennyson

It little profits that an idle king,
By this still hearth, among these barren crags,
Match'd with an aged wife, I mete and dole
Unequal laws unto a savage race,
That hoard, and sleep, and feed, and know not me.

I cannot rest from travel: I will drink
Life to the lees: all times I have enjoy'd
Greatly, have suffer'd greatly, both with those
That loved me, and alone; on shore, and when
Thro' scudding drifts the rainy Hyades
Vest the dim sea: I am become a name;
For always roaming with a hungry heart
Much have I seen and known; cities of men
And manners, climates, councils, governments,
Myself not least, but honour'd of them all;
And drunk delight of battle with my peers;
Far on the ringing plains of windy Troy.
I am part of all that I have met;
Yet all experience is an arch wherethro'
Gleams that untravell'd world, whose margin fades
For ever and for ever when I move.
How dull it is to pause, to make an end,

To rust unburnish'd, not to shine in use!
As tho' to breathe were life. Life piled on life
Were all too little, and of one to me
Little remains: but every hour is saved
From that eternal silence, something more,
A bringer of new things; and vile it were
For some three suns to store and hoard myself,
And this gray spirit yearning in desire
To follow knowledge like a sinking star,
Beyond the utmost bound of human thought.

This is my son, mine own Telemachus,
To whom I leave the sceptre and the isle—
Well-loved of me, discerning to fulfil
This labour, by slow prudence to make mild
A rugged people, and thro' soft degrees
Subdue them to the useful and the good.
Most blameless is he, centred in the sphere
Of common duties, decent not to fail
In offices of tenderness, and pay
Meet adoration to my household gods,
When I am gone. He works his work, I mine.

There lies the port; the vessel puffs her sail:
There gloom the dark broad seas. My mariners,
Souls that have toil'd, and wrought, and thought with me—
That ever with a frolic welcome took
The thunder and the sunshine, and opposed
Free hearts, free foreheads—you and I are old;
Old age had yet his honour and his toil;
Death closes all: but something ere the end,
Some work of noble note, may yet be done,
Not unbecoming men that strove with Gods.
The lights begin to twinkle from the rocks:
The long day wanes: the slow moon climbs: the deep
Moans round with many voices. Come, my friends,
'Tis not too late to seek a newer world.
Push off, and sitting well in order smite
The sounding furrows; for my purpose holds
To sail beyond the sunset, and the baths
Of all the western stars, until I die.

It may be that the gulfs will wash us down:
It may be we shall touch the Happy Isles,
And see the great Achilles, whom we knew.

Tho' much is taken, much abides; and tho'
We are not now that strength which in the old days
Moved earth and heaven; that which we are, we are;
One equal-temper of heroic hearts,
Made weak by time and fate, but strong in will
To strive, to seek, to find, and not to yield.

Other contemporary poems with allusions to *The Odyssey* include:

"Siren Song" by Margaret Atwood

"Calipso" by Suzanne Vega

"The Cyclops in the Ocean" by Nikki Giovanni

"An Ancient Gesture" by Edna St. Vincent Millay

"Penelope" by Carol Ann Duffy

"The Sea Call" by Nikos Kazantzakis

"Circe's Power" by Louise Gluck

"Daughter Moon" by Diane Wakoski

"Ithaca" by C. P. Cavafy

With permission from Macmillan Publishers, here is a contemporary take on Penelope by the British poet, Carol Ann Duffy. It is from a collection of poems called *The World's Wife*, which includes the voices of Mrs. Midas, Mrs. Tiresias, Mrs. Sisyphus, and Medusa.

PENELOPE

by Carol Ann Duffy

At first, I looked along the road
hoping to see him saunter home
among the olive trees,

a whistle for the dog
who mourned him with his warm head on my knees.
Six months of this
and then I noticed that whole days had passed
without my noticing.
I sorted cloth and scissors, needle, thread,

thinking to amuse myself,
but found a lifetime's industry instead.
I sewed a girl
under a single star—cross-stitch, silver silk—
running after childhood's bouncing ball.
I chose between three greens for the grass;
a smoky pink, a shadow's grey
to show a snapdragon gargling a bee.
I threaded walnut brown for a tree,

my thimble like an acorn
pushing up through umber soil.
Beneath the shade
I wrapped a maiden in a deep embrace
with heroism's boy
and lost myself completely
in a wild embroidery of love, lust, loss, lessons learnt;
then watched him sail away
into the loose gold stitching of the sun.

And when the others came to take his place,
disturb my peace,
I played for time.
I wore a widow's face, kept my head down,
did my work by day, at night unpicked it.
I knew which hour of the dark the moon
would start to fray,
I stitched it.
Grey threads and brown

pursued my needle's leaping fish
to form a river that would never reach the sea.
I tricked it. I was picking out
the smile of a woman at the centre

of this world, self-contained, absorbed, content,
most certainly not waiting,
when I heard a far-too-late familiar tread outside the door.
I licked my scarlet thread
and aimed it surely at the middle of the needle's eye once more.

In our discussion of this poem and others, I try to persuade students that their newly acquired knowledge of *The Odyssey* is something that will stay with them forever and enrich their reading of many other texts. To emphasize this point throughout the year, I ask students to compare characters across texts: for example, Odysseus with Beowulf or Odysseus with Cyrano de Bergerac (see Figure 6.9). After students have constructed these Venn diagrams of the characters' similarities and differences, I ask them to consider with whom they would prefer to dine. No one ever chooses Beowulf.

FIGURE 6.9   Comparing Heroes

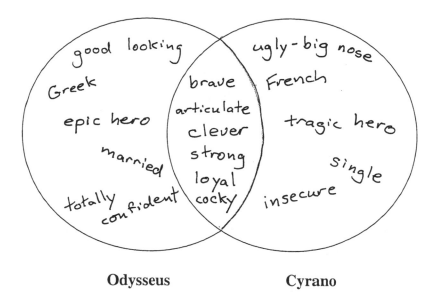

Odysseus   **Cyrano**

Literature, Knowledge, and the High School Graduate

SUPERMODEL LINDA EVANGELISTA once remarked that "It was God who made me so beautiful. If I weren't, then I'd be a teacher." Now, I have never strolled down a runway and so may be quite mistaken, but it seems to me that teaching requires a great deal more divine intervention than wearing beautiful clothes beautifully. Some days imparting even one thing to one child feels like a minor miracle. And as the days count down to graduation, the urgency to work miracles increases. Eighteen states require students to pass exit exams in order to earn a diploma. To the extent that these tests help ensure that every student has had access to a rigorous curriculum, I applaud them. A high school diploma should represent not just time spent at a desk but a body of knowledge and set of skills that students have mastered. Assessing students' progress toward these standards makes sense. Unfortunately, too often exit exams punish students for the failings of their schools. Linda Evangelista may have insight into how to teach children, and were she not so beautiful perhaps education would benefit enormously from her contribution. She should know, however, that even greater demands would be made on her.

THE AMERICAN DIPLOMA PROJECT

In 2003 a group calling itself The American Diploma Project sought to create a set of standards describing what high school graduates should know and be able to do. Their goal was to bring consistency to requirements for graduation and incorporate into the document the expectations of the business community. To write the benchmarks, they tapped the expertise of high school teachers, college professors, and leaders from industry. Though instinctively suspicious of anyone outside education telling me what I should be doing in the classroom, I was encouraged by this initiative because the mobile nature of our society demands greater consistency across the land. While state standards are moving toward a common language, national standards are still a long way off and may never become a reality without a national exam.

The American Diploma Project benchmark for writing about literature reads: "A high school graduate should be able to analyze the complexity of moral dilemmas in historically significant works of literature, as revealed by characters' motivation and behavior." In order to reach this standard students need to be able to read and analyze literature in which characters confront moral dilemmas and explain how the characters' words and actions reveal their struggle. Among the academic expectations subsumed in this skill are the abilities to:

- read historically significant works of literature with comprehension and insight;
- recognize how authors use imagery, syntax, and diction to reveal character and advance a theme;

- construct a thesis that expresses an understanding of the moral dilemma and establishes a point of view;
- cite appropriate evidence from the literary text to illuminate and defend their analysis;
- connect this evidence to the thesis; and
- demonstrate control of Standard English through the correct use of grammar, punctuation, capitalization, spelling, and paragraph and sentence structure.

In order for students to meet such a benchmark by the end of twelfth grade, they need practice with literary analysis throughout middle and high school. Writing assignments that ask students to compose imaginary letters to characters or create new endings may engage students in thinking about literature and result in written products, but they do not prepare students for analysis. Some argue that only students bent on pursuing careers in university English departments—a small subset indeed—need to develop the ability to analyze literature. But, surely this is important training for every mind. Literature frequently provides a context in which to examine moral dilemmas. As students grapple with the decisions characters make they explore their own values.

TEACHING *JULIUS CAESAR*

While working through *Julius Caesar,* I ask tenth-grade students to consider the funeral orations of Brutus and Antony and write an analytical essay of approximately 700–1,000 words in which they compare and contrast the speeches' rhetorical effectiveness. Which has the more powerful effect on the Roman mob? What is it about the speaker's word choice and oratorical style that accomplishes this? I want students to identify and analyze the persuasive techniques that Brutus and Antony employ and offer evidence to support their interpretations. I remind them to make detailed references to the text.

Brutus' Funeral Oration

Be patient till the last.

Romans, countrymen, and lovers! hear me for my cause, and be silent, that you may hear: believe me for mine honour, and have respect to mine honour, that you may believe: censure me in your wisdom, and awake your senses, that you may the better judge. If there be any in this assembly, any dear friend of Caesar's, to him I say, that Brutus' love to Caesar was no less than his. If then that friend demand why Brutus rose against Caesar, this is my answer: —Not that I loved Caesar less, but that I loved Rome more. Had you rather Caesar were living and die all slaves, than that Caesar were dead, to live all free men? As Caesar loved me, I weep for him; as he was fortunate, I rejoice at it; as he was valiant, I honour him: but, as he was ambitious, I slew him. There is tears for his love; joy for his fortune; honour for his valour; and death for his ambition. Who is here so base that would be a bondman? If any, speak; for him have I offended.

Who is here so rude that would not be a Roman? If any, speak; for him have I offended. Who is here so vile that will not love his country? If any, speak; for him have I offended. I pause for a reply. (III.ii)

Antony's Funeral Oration

Friends, Romans, countrymen, lend me your ears;
I come to bury Caesar, not to praise him.
The evil that men do lives after them;
The good is oft interred with their bones;

So let it be with Caesar. The noble Brutus
Hath told you Caesar was ambitious:
If it were so, it was a grievous fault,
And grievously hath Caesar answer'd it.
Here, under leave of Brutus and the rest—
For Brutus is an honourable man;
So are they all; all honourable men—
Come I to speak in Caesar's funeral.
He was my friend, faithful and just to me:
But Brutus says he was ambitious;
And Brutus is an honourable man.
He hath brought many captives home to Rome
Whose ransoms did the general coffers fill:
Did this in Caesar seem ambitious?
When that the poor have cried, Caesar hath wept:
Ambition should be made of sterner stuff:
Yet Brutus says he was ambitious;
And Brutus is an honourable man.
You all did see that on the Lupercal
I thrice presented him a kingly crown,
Which he did thrice refuse: was this ambition?
Yet Brutus says he was ambitious;
And, sure, he is an honourable man.
I speak not to disprove what Brutus spoke,
But here I am to speak what I do know.
You all did love him once, not without cause:
What cause withholds you then, to mourn for him?
O judgment! thou art fled to brutish beasts,
And men have lost their reason. Bear with me;
My heart is in the coffin there with Caesar,
And I must pause till it come back to me. (III.ii)

Both speeches are rhetorically effective, but while Brutus appeals to the crowd's reason, Antony appeals to their emotions. Given the character of the Roman populace (or any mob), it is no surprise that Antony's methods are the more effective. Brutus makes use of isocolon—successive phrases or clauses of approximately equal length:

- "Hear me for my cause, and be silent, that you may hear."
- "Believe me for mine honor, and have respect to mine honor, that you may believe."
- "Censure me in your wisdom, and awake your senses, that you may the better judge."

The symmetry of these lines mirrors the logical approach that Brutus takes with the people. He reasons with them. Later in the oration he employs alliteration, which suggests the inevitability of his reasoning: "Who is here so base that would be a bondman?" and "Who is here so rude that would not be a Roman?" The parallel sentence structures of these lines also lend power to his argument. When Brutus steps down, the crowd is entirely on his side.

While Brutus' speech was written in prose, Antony's is in verse. Antony uses a variety of rhetorical and poetic devices to sway the crowd from Brutus' point of view and toward his own. Antony employs antithesis, turning words into the reverse of what they normally mean. He assures the crowd that Brutus is "an honourable man; / So are they All; All honourable men." Using the phrase as a refrain, Antony turns the word "honourable" into an insult. Another powerful rhetorical device is his use of paralipsis, pretending to pass over a matter while really stressing it: "It is not meet you know how Caesar loved you," "'Tis good you know not that you are his heirs." Antony appeals to the mob's basest emotions: greed, fear, and a love of violence.

Such an essay poses fundamental difficulties for students unused to such analysis. Yet the recognition of rhetorical devices has value and, with scaffolding from teacher and peers, most students can produce an essay that demonstrates an emerging understanding of the speeches' structure. These essays are not the most original papers students write in the course of the year, but they often demonstrate a leap forward in terms of students' understanding of how to write about literature. They are forced to look closely at the speakers' word choice and their appeals to emotion. I hope that through the process students will recognize rhetoric and become less vulnerable to manipulation. This flows from the requirement to think analytically and to marshal thoughts in an organized fashion. Although this is a demanding assignment, the ability to construct such an argument is a highly desirable skill that all graduating seniors should possess.

Applying Literature to Life

A common student complaint when reading a classic is that the text is irrelevant to their lives. "Mrs. Jago, why are we always reading about all these old guys?" Reminding them that both Telemachos and Beowulf were quite young does little to stem the revolt. Instead I look for ways to engage students in lessons where they apply what they have learned from literature to more familiar circumstances, for example an election. As our study of *Julius Caesar* draws to a close, I ask students to consider who would make the best president: Antony, Caesar, Brutus, or Cassius. Before opening the floor for discussion, I ask them to select their candidate and list the reasons for their choices. The results are fascinating. Each candidate seems to draw particular voters. The evidence students cite to support their choice reveals a great deal about what individual students are looking for in a leader. As students argue, they begin to see how others think about the kinds of people we choose to entrust with power.

A Note on Consistency

This same idea could be adapted as a writing task. Last year when I realized that I hadn't yet assigned a persuasive essay and that my tenth-grade students might be asked to produce one for California's exit exam, I adapted this lesson for their January final exam. It might appear from the way I present teaching ideas in this book that I have a set way of teaching particular texts. In fact, just as no two groups of students are ever quite the same, no two years proceed in exactly the same fashion. I would like to believe that I am always improving my practice, but in fact I often make adaptations that I later abandon. Teaching is an organic process. This is one of the things that make it such a challenging profession.

Writing a persuasive essay about Julius Caesar

Who would make the best president: Antony, Brutus, Cassius, or Caesar? In a fully developed persuasive essay, explain your choice using examples from the play. Be sure to offer evidence of the character traits that led to your choice.

You may use your book or any notes you have taken. Remember to make reference to why someone else might think otherwise.

Papers due at the end of the period.

In many ways it is Brutus, not Caesar, who is the tragic hero of this play. Like Hamlet, he has a divided spirit. Brutus' commitment to serving the Roman people and the Republic is always first in his heart, yet he hesitates to harm the friend who has been so good to him. He ponders long into the night and tries to justify the assassination. Cassius is able to manipulate Brutus precisely because Brutus is so noble and thoughtful. Brutus is too high-minded to see that the noble Cassius is actually motivated by jealousy. Caesar had seen this all along, and had spotted Cassius' "lean and hungry look" early in the play. In the final scene of Act V, Antony calls Brutus, "the noblest Roman of them all."

> All the conspirators save only he
> Did that they did in envy of great Caesar;
> He only, in a general honest thought
> And common good to all, made one of them.
> His life was gentle, and the elements
> So mix'd in him that Nature might stand up
> And say to all the world, "This was a man!" (V.v)

But would such a man make the best president?

Assessing Student Effort

This election lesson incorporates key elements of successful literature study:

- Close reading of the text
- Character analysis
- Drawing inferences
- Application
- Evaluation

These are also the skills most commonly assessed on standardized tests. Students who have varied opportunities to practice these skills—whether through class discussion, writing assignments, or group presentations—should be able to answer correctly the artificial multiple-choice questions that test publishers throw at them. I would never waste valuable preparation time writing multiple-choice questions, compiling character identification lists, or composing true/false questions for an assessment of our classroom literature. You can find such items for almost any classic on the Internet or in published study guides. Moreover students will invariably point out how my homemade multiple-choice questions are vaguely expressed and defend their incorrect answers with reason. I give up. Occasionally I will use a packaged test for review purposes, putting students to work in groups and accepting only scores of 100 percent (after about a half an hour, I let them use their books). More valuable for classroom assessment is the kind of test that offers students choice in terms of how they demonstrate what they have learned.

Test on Julius Caesar.   Please answer five of the following questions in well-developed paragraphs. You may not use your books. Papers are due at the end of the period.

1. In your opinion, is Julius Caesar or Brutus the tragic hero of this play? Defend your answer with specific references. Demonstrate that you know the characteristics of a tragic hero.
2. Do you agree or disagree with this analysis of Brutus by E. M. Forster? Explain. *Brutus is an intellectual who can do things, who is not hampered by doubts. He cannot realize that men seek their own interests for he has never sought his own, has lived nobly among noble thoughts, wedded to a noble wife.*
3. Why was Antony's funeral oration so much more effective than Brutus'? What did he understand about the Roman mob that Brutus didn't?
4. Describe the relationship between Cassius and Brutus.
5. Why did Cassius tell Brutus that "The fault, dear Brutus, is not in the stars but in ourselves"?

6. Explain what Brutus meant when he said in Act V, "O Julius Caesar, thou art mighty yet;/ Thy spirit walks abroad and turns our swords / In our own proper entrails."

7. How docs Shakespeare make the common people (the mob) seem less than noble in his play *Julius Caesar*?

8. Describe three errors of judgment that Brutus makes in the course of the play.

9. At the play's conclusion, it is clear that Octavius will be the new ruler of Rome. What type of leader do you think he will be? Defend your answer.

This kind of test is relatively easy to grade. I read the papers quickly, primarily for content, identifying as I read outstanding answers. The next day in class we walk through the test question by question, and I call on students to read aloud model responses. This helps those who have received only partial credit to understand why without my having to mark papers with a lot of explanation.

This kind of classroom assessment holds students individually accountable for their reading. Concerns about plagiarism have made many teachers reluctant to assign grades solely on the basis of student essays. Various online services now allow teachers to catch students who copy text from Internet sources, but I would rather put my energy elsewhere. I check for authenticity by requiring drafts with final copies of essays. A test like this one, made up of a list of discussion questions, measures students' comprehension of the literature separate from their writing skills. Clearly the ability to write well allows some students to articulate their understanding more effectively, but such an assessment allows students with emerging writing skills, for example English language learners, to earn a high grade for comprehension without sophisticated writing skills.

I avoid group projects for assessment because almost invariably they allow some students to slack off while others—the ones who care most about the grade—do all the work. No matter how cunningly I craft a scoring guide it is still hard to hold individuals as accountable as I would like when students work as a team. In, for example, an M.B.A. course there is a fundamental need for group effort, but at this stage of a child's education, I want to know how well each student has understood the text. I need to hear from each one separately.

STUDYING CLASSICAL LITERATURE FOR A BRAVE NEW WORLD

In Act V, scene i of *The Tempest* the youthful Miranda is amazed to discover more of these wondrous creatures called "man."

> Miranda: O, wonder!
> How many goodly creatures are there here!
> How beauteous mankind is! O brave new world,
> That has such people in't!
> Prospero: 'Tis new to thee.
>   (V. i)

It is my hope that students will be similarly enchanted by their acquaintance with classics like *The Odyssey, Julius Caesar,* and *Crime and Punishment.* It is my experience that they relish the discovery of other "goodly" books they can now read if not with ease, with comprehension. They will have acquired the tools necessary for negotiating complex works. Like Prospero, Miranda's wizard of a father, teachers need to create an environment that will nurture this. To wring one's hand and complain that kids these days do not have the temperament for long books not only is fruitless but also denies students an opportunity to develop what may become a joy for life. Literature lessons must recognize and confront the challenges that classics pose for young readers. I have tried to offer engaging and intellectually rigorous ways of doing this in the classroom. Playing games with the classics accomplishes nothing. In the brave new world that I envision, students will graduate from high school able to read and understand the best that literature has to offer. They will also be exposed to ideas and values outside their realm of experience. In the process students discover the heroic dimension of their own lives.

Recommended Classic Texts

GRADES 6–7

Alice in Wonderland and *Through the Looking Glass,* Lewis Carroll
Anne of Green Gables, Lucy Maud Montgomery
The Arabian Nights, selected tales
Blue Willow, Doris Gates
Boy: Tales of Childhood, Roald Dahl
Caddie Woodlawn, Carol Ryrie Brink
A Christmas Carol, Charles Dickens
Heidi, Johanna Spyri
Island of the Blue Dolphins, Scott O'Dell
Journey to Topaz, Yoshiko Uchida
The Jungle Book, Rudyard Kipling
Kidnapped, Robert Louis Stevenson
Little Women, Louisa May Alcott

The Lion, the Witch, and the Wardrobe, C. S. Lewis
The Legend of Sleepy Hollow, Washington Irving
Little House on the Prairie, Laura Ingalls Wilder
The Martian Chronicles, Ray Bradbury
Old Possum's Book of Practical Cats, T. S. Eliot
Out of the Dust, Karen Hesse
Peter Pan, James Barrie
The Pearl, John Steinbeck
The People Could Fly, Virginia Hamilton
The Secret Garden, Frances Hodgson Burnett
The Story of My Life, Helen Keller
Tales from Shakespeare, Charles and Mary Lamb
Tuck Everlasting, Natalie Babbitt
White Fang, Jack London
The Wizard of Oz, L. Frank Baum
Watership Down, Richard Adams
The Wind in the Willows, Kenneth Grahame
A Wrinkle in Time, Madeleine L'Engle
The Yearling, Marjorie Kinnan Rawlings
Zlateh the Goat and Other Stories, Isaac Bashevis Singer

GRADES 7–9

All Creatures Great and Small, James Herriot
Animal Farm, George Orwell
Autobiography of Miss Jane Pittman, Ernest J. Gaines
Buried Onions, Gary Soto
The Call of the Wild, Jack London
Cold Sassy Tree, Olive Ann Burns

The Count of Monte Cristo, Alexander Dumas

The Diary of a Young Girl, Anne Frank

Fahrenheit 451, Ray Bradbury

Flowers for Algernon, Daniel Keyes

The Good Earth, Pearl S. Buck

Great Expectations, Charles Dickens

The Heart Is a Lonely Hunter, Carson McCullers

Hiroshima, John Hersey

House on Mango Street, Sandra Cisneros

If Beale Street Could Talk, James Baldwin

The Lord of the Flies, William Golding

The Lord of the Rings, J. R. R. Tolkien

The Metamorphosis, Franz Kafka

Of Mice and Men, John Steinbeck

A Midsummer Night's Dream, William Shakespeare

Mythology, Edith Hamilton

Night, Elie Wiesel

Pygmalion, Bernard Shaw

A Raisin in the Sun, Lorraine Hansberry

"The Raven," Edgar Allan Poe

A Separate Peace, John Knowles

Sherlock Holmes stories, Sir Arthur Conan Doyle

Shoeless Joe, Ray Kinsella

The Strange Case of Dr. Jekyll and Mr. Hyde, Robert Louis Stevenson

The Sound of Waves, Yukio Mishima

To Be a Slave, Julius Lester

A Tree Grows in Brooklyn, Betty Smith

To Kill a Mockingbird, Harper Lee

Tom Sawyer, Mark Twain

Twelfth Night, William Shakespeare

War of the Worlds, H. G. Wells

GRADES 9–10

1984, George Orwell

All Quiet on the Western Front, Erich Maria Remarque

The Assistant, Bernard Malamud

The Ballad of the Sad Café, Carson McCullers

Beowulf

Black Boy, Richard Wright

Bless Me, Ultima, Rudolfo Anaya

The Bluest Eye, Toni Morrison

Brave New World, Aldous Huxley

A Canticle for Leibowitz, Walter Miller

The Catcher in the Rye, J. D. Salinger

The Chosen, Chaim Potok

Cyrano de Bergerac, Edmund Rostand

Dead Souls, Nicolai Gogol

Deerslayer, James Fenimore Cooper

Doctor Zhivago, Boris Pasternack

A Doll's House, Henrik Ibsen

Emma, Jane Austen

"The Fall of the House of Usher," Edgar Allan Poe

Fences, August Wilson

Ficciones, Jorge Luis Borges

Frankenstein, Mary Shelley

Grendel, John Gardner

The Hunchback of Notre Dame, Victor Hugo

The Iliad, Homer

Ivanhoe, Sir Walter Scott

Jane Eyre, Charlotte Brontë

Julius Caesar, William Shakespeare

The Jungle, Upton Sinclair

"Master Harold" . . . and the Boys, Athol Fugard

Le Morte D'Arthur, Thomas Malory

Malgudi Days, R. K. Narayan

Much Ado About Nothing, William Shakespeare

My Antonia, Willa Cather

The Natural, Bernard Malamud

Obasan, Joy Kogawa

The Odyssey, Homer

The Old Man and the Sea, Ernest Hemingway

Oliver Twist, Charles Dickens

The Once and Future King, T. H. White

One Day in the Life of Ivan Denisovich, Alexander Solzhenitsyn

The Ox-Bow Incident, Walter Van Tilburg Clark

Our Town, Thornton Wilder

The Picture of Dorian Gray, Oscar Wilde

Romeo and Juliet, William Shakespeare

The Secret Life of Walter Mitty, James Thurber

Sense and Sensibility, Jane Austen

Scent of Apples, Bienvenido N. Santos

Silent Spring, Rachel Carson

The Souls of Black Folk, W. E. B. DuBois

The Stranger, Albert Camus

A Tale of Two Cities, Charles Dickens

Things Fall Apart, Chinua Achebe

The Woman Warrior, Maxine Hong Kingston

Wuthering Heights, Emily Brontë

GRADES 11–12

The Adventures of Huckleberry Finn, Mark Twain

The Aeneid, Virgil

The Age of Innocence, Edith Wharton

Autobiography, Benjamin Franklin

The Baron in the Trees, Italo Calvino

Beloved, Toni Morrison

Billy Budd, Herman Melville

Blindness, José Saramago

The Canterbury Tales, Geoffrey Chaucer

Candide, Voltaire

Catch-22, Joseph Heller

Chronicle of a Death Foretold, Gabriel García Márquez

The Crucible, Arthur Miller

Cry, the Beloved Country, Alan Paton

Ceremony, Leslie Marmon Silko

Crime and Punishment, Fyodor Dostoyevsky

A Death in the Family, James Agee

Death of a Salesman, Arthur Miller

Democracy, Joan Didion

Democracy in America, Alexis de Tocqueville

A Farewell to Arms, Ernest Hemingway

Giants in the Earth, O. E. Rolvaag

The Glass Menagerie, Tennessee Williams

The Grapes of Wrath, John Steinbeck

The Great Gatsby, F. Scott Fitzgerald

Hamlet, William Shakespeare

Hard Times, Charles Dickens

Heart of Darkness, Joseph Conrad

A House for Mr. Biswas, V. S. Naipaul

The House of Seven Gables, Nathaniel Hawthorne

If Not Now, When?, Primo Levi

The Inferno, Dante

Invisible Man, Ralph Ellison

July's People, Nadine Gordimer

Leaves of Grass, Walt Whitman

The Left Hand of Darkness, Madeleine L'Engle

The Lost Steps, Alejo Carpentier

Macbeth, William Shakespeare

Madame Bovary, Gustave Flaubert

Moby Dick, Herman Melville

"A Modest Proposal," Jonathan Swift

Native Son, Richard Wright

The Old Gringo, Carlos Fuentes

One Hundred Years of Solitude, Gabriel García Márquez

Narrative of the Life of Frederick Douglass, Frederick Douglass

Palace Walk, Naguib Mahfouz

The Piano Lesson, August Wilson

Pilgrim at Tinker Creek, Annie Dillard

The Plague, Albert Camus

A Portrait of the Artist as a Young Man, James Joyce

Pride and Prejudice, Jane Austen

The Prince, Niccolo Machiavelli

The Red Badge of Courage, Stephen Crane

The Return of the Native, Thomas Hardy

Rosencrantz and Guildenstern Are Dead, Tom Stoppard

Sacred Hunger, Barry Unsworth

The Same Sea, Amos Oz

The Scarlet Letter, Nathaniel Hawthorne

Song of Solomon, Toni Morrison

The Sound and the Fury, William Faulkner

The Theban Plays, Sophocles

Their Eyes Were Watching God, Zora Neal Hurston

The Things They Carried, Tim O'Brien

To the Lighthouse, Virginia Woolf

Up from Slavery, Booker T. Washington

Walden, Henry David Thoreau

Waiting for the Barbarians, J. M. Coetzee

Winesburg, Ohio, Sherwood Anderson

Appendix B

Classic Bestsellers

Book magazine (July/August 2003) published the following list of "classic" bestsellers. While I would argue that any title published as recently as 1997 can hardly be labeled a classic, the results of their survey are fascinating. Though the numbers of copies sold are obviously influenced by teachers assigning certain common texts, it is amazing to see how well classical literature continues to sell.

Rank/Title	Number of copies sold in 2002
1 *The Hobbit* (1937)	542,000
2 *The Catcher in the Rye* (1951)	524,000
3 *The Red Tent* (1997)	500,000
4 *To Kill a Mockingbird* (1960)	462,000
5 *Lord of the Flies* (1954)	226,000
6 *The Great Gatsby* (1925)	223,000

7	*Of Mice and Men* (1937)	219,000
8	*1984* (1949)	217,000
9	*Fahrenheit 451* (1953)	212,000
10	*Animal Farm* (1945)	192,000
11	*The Grapes of Wrath*	164,000
12	*The Silmarillion* (1977)	162,000
13	*Memoirs of a Geisha* (1997)	146,000
14	*The Adventures of Huckleberry Finn* (1885)	144,000
15	*Brave New World* (1932)	135,000
16	*The Scarlet Letter* (1850)	133,000
17	*The Alchemist* (1988)	132,000
18	*The Old Man and the Sea* (1952)	131,000
19	*Atlas Shrugged* (1957)	130,000
20	*A Separate Peace* (1959)	122,000
21	*She's Come Undone* (1992)	117,000
22	*Catch-22* (1961)	116,000
23	*The House on Mango Street* (1984)	114,000
24	*A Tree Grows in Brooklyn* (1943)	114,000
25	*Pride and Prejudice* (1813)	113,000
26	*Siddhartha* (1951)	108,000
27	*The Clan of the Cave Bear* (1980)	105,000
28	*The Pearl* (1947)	103,000
29	*Slaughterhouse-Five* (1969)	101,000
30	*Frankenstein* (1818)	96,000
31	*All Quiet on the Western Front* (1929)	96,000
32	*A Tale of Two Cities* (1859)	92,000
33	*Their Eyes Were Watching God* (1937)	88,000
34	*Heart of Darkness* (1902)	87,000
35	*The Fountainhead* (1943)	81,000
36	*The Things They Carried* (1990)	77,000
37	*Possession* (1990)	75,000

38	*The Awakening* (1899)	74,000
39	*And Then There Were None* (1939)	73,000
40	*Great Expectations* (1861)	72,000
41	*Jane Eyre* (1847)	72,000
42	*A Farewell to Arms* (1929)	72,000
43	*Wuthering Heights* (1847)	71,000
44	*One Hundred Years of Solitude* (1967)	70,000
45	*Watership Down* (1972)	70,000
46	*The Chosen* (1967)	70,000
47	*The Sun Also Rises* (1926)	68,000
48	*Dune* (1965)	66,000
49	*Invisible Man* (1952)	65,000
50	*Interview with a Vampire* (1976)	65,000

Source: Nielsen BookScan, based on sales data from January 1, 2002, to December 31, 2002, at chain bookstores and other outlets including Amazon.com. It does not measure sales at high school or college bookstores. The list ranks books that are at least five years old.

Works Cited

Abrams, M. H. 1999. *A Glossary of Literary Terms.* 7th ed. Boston: Heinle & Heinle.

Applebee, A. N. 1989. "A Study of Book-Length Works Taught in High school English Programs," Report Number 1.2. Albany, NY: Center for the Learning and Teaching of Literature.

Beck, I., and M. McKeown. 1981. "Developing Questions That Promote Comprehension: The Story Map." *Language Arts* (November/December): 913–18.

Beck, I. L., M. McKeown, and L. Kucan. 2002. *Bringing Words to Life: Robust Vocabulary Instruction.* New York: The Guilford Press.

Bernstein, C. 2003. "The Difficult Poem." *Harper's*, June, 24–25.

Berthoff, W. 1986. *Literature and the Continuances of Virtue.* Princeton, NJ: Princeton University Press.

Birkerts, S. 1994. *The Gutenberg Elegies: The Fate of Reading in an Electronic Age.* Boston: Faber and Faber.

———, ed. 1996. *Literature, The Evolving Canon*. 2d ed. Boston: Allyn and Bacon.

Bradford, Ernle. 1963. *Ulysses Found*. New York: Harcourt, Brace & World.

Calvino, Italo. 1999. *Why Read the Classics?* New York: Pantheon Books.

Carey. S. 1978. "The Child as Word Learner." In *Linguistic Theory and Psychological Reality*, edited by M. Halle, J. Bresnan, and G. A. Miller, 264–93. Cambridge, MA: MIT Press.

Chall, J. S., and V. A. Jacobs. 1996. "The Reading, Writing, and Language Connection." In *Literacy and Education: Essays in Memory of Dina Feitelson*, edited by J. Shimron, 33–48. Cresskill, NJ: Hampton Press.

Dale, E., and J. O'Rourke. 1986. *Vocabulary Building*. Columbus, OH: Zaner-Bloser.

D'Souza, D. 2003. *Letters to a Young Conservative*. New York: Basic Books.

Duffy, Carol Anne. 1999. *The World's Wife*. London: MacMillan.

Eco, Umberto. 1994. *Six Walks in the Fictional Woods*. Cambridge, MA: Harvard University Press.

English-Language Arts Content Standards for California Public Schools. 1997. California Department of Education.

Frye, Northrop. 1957. *Anatomy of Criticism: Four Essays*. Princeton, NJ: Princeton University Press.

Fuerbringer, J. 2003. "Bets in Both Directions Help a Fund Look Good." *New York Times* 27, April, 7.

Goldberg, M. 2001. "An Interview with Linda Darling-Hammond: Balanced Optimism." *Phi Delta Kappan* 82 (9): 687–90.

Grahame, K. 1983. *The Wind in the Willows*. Middlesex, England: Penguin Books.

Graves, M. F., G. J. Burnetti, and W. H. Slater. 1982. "The Reading Vocabularies of Primary-Grade Children of Varying Geographic and Social Backgrounds." In *New Inquiries in Reading Research and Instruction*, edited by J. A. Harris and L. A. Harris, 99–104. Rochester, NY: National Reading Conference.

Hart, B., and T. R. Risley. 2003. "The Early Catastrophe: The 30 Million Word Gap by Age 3." *American Educator* (spring).

Hollander, J. 2001. *Sonnets: From Dante to the Present.* Everyman's Library Pocket Poetry collection. New York: Alfred A. Knopf.

Homer. 1967a. *The Odyssey.* Translated by Albert Cook. New York: W. W. Norton and Company.

———. 1967b. *The Odyssey.* Translated by Richmond Latimore. New York: Harper Perrenial.

———. 1998. *The Odyssey.* Translated by Robert Fitzgerald. New York: Noonday Press.

Housman, A. E. 1987. *The Collected Poems of A. E. Housman.* New York: Henry Holt.

London, J. 1981. *The Call of the Wild, White Fang, and Other Stories.* New York: Penguin Books.

Mandler, J., and N. Johnson. 1977. "Rememberance of Things Parsed: Story Structure and Recall." *Cognitive Psychology* 9: 111–51.

Massachusetts English Language Arts Standards. 1997. Boston: Massachusetts Department of Education.

Matthews, Brander. 1914. *Oxford Book of American Essays.* London: Oxford Press.

McKibben, B. 2003. "Keep Us Human." *Los Angeles Times,* Opinion, 14 April.

Nagy, W. E., R. C. Anderson., and P. A. Herman. 1987. "Learning Word Meanings from Context During Normal Reading." *American Educational Research Journal* 23: 237–70.

Nussbaum, M. C. 1995. *Poetic Justice.* Boston: Beacon Press.

Oliver, M. 1998. *Rules for the Dance: A Handbook for Writing and Reading Metrical Verse.* New York: Houghton Mifflin.

Poe, E. A. 1984. *Poe, Poetry and Tales.* New York: The Library of America.

Pressley, M., C. J. Johnson., S. Symons., J. S. McGoldrick., and J. A. Kurita. 1989. "Strategies That Improve Children's Memory and Comprehension of Text." *The Elementary School Journal* 90: 3–32.

Rosenblatt, L. M. 1983. *Literature as Exploration.* New York: The Modern Language Association.

Rumelhart, D. 1975. "Notes on a Schema for Stories." In *Representation and Understanding*, edited by D. G. Browbrow and Allan Collins, 211–36. New York: Academic Press.

Shelley, M. 1988. *Frankenstein.* New York: Perma-Bound Classics.

Smith, J. B., B. Smith, and A. S. Bryk. 1998. *Setting the Pace: Opportunities to Learn in Chicago's Elementary Schools.* Chicago: Consortium on Chicago School Research.

Smith, M. K. 1941. "Measurement of the Size of General English Vocabulary Through the Elementary Grades and High School." *Genetic Psychological Monographs* 24: 311–45.

Stahl, S. A., and T. G. Shiel. 1992. "Teaching Meaning Vocabulary: Productive Approaches for Poor Readers." *Reading and Writing Quarterly: Overcoming Learning Disabilities* 8: 223–41.

Steinbeck, J. 1999. *The Grapes of Wrath.* New York: Penguin Books.

Stevenson, R. L. 1979. *The Strange Case of Dr. Jekyll and Mr. Hyde.* New York: Penguin Books.

Stigler, J. W., and J. Hiebert. 1999. *The Teaching Gap: Best Ideas from the World's Teachers for Improving Education in the Classroom.* New York: The Free Press.

Tolstoy, L. 1960. *The Death of Ivan Ilych and Other Stories.* New York: Signet Classics.

Willingham, D. T. 2003. "Students Remember . . . What They Think About." *American Educator* (spring): 37–41.

Willis, S. 2002. "An Interview with James Stigler: Creating a Knowledge Base for Teaching." *Educational Leadership* 59 (6): 6–11.

Wolff, T. 2003 "Class Picture." *The New Yorker,* 6 January, 71.

Wright, R. 1979. *Native Son.* New York: Perennial Classics.

Vygotsky, L. S. 1962. *Thought and Language.* Edited and translated by E. Hanfmann and G. Vakar. Cambridge, MA: MIT Press.

Zanoza, M. 2003. "Oprah's Book Club Past, Present, and Future." *Book,* May/June,13.

Index